With
FORKED
TONGUES

TO JUDITH

With FORKED TONGUES

WHAT ARE NATIONAL LANGUAGES GOOD FOR?

Edited by
FLORIAN COULMAS

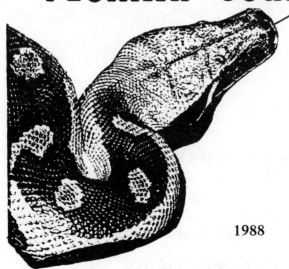

1988

KAROMA  PUBLISHERS, INC.

1988

Paper Only
Printed in the Republic of Singapore.

ISBN 0-89720-084-5

Contents

Preface

> I wrote a book in which I was talking about nationalism, and I said, "There is, of course, one nation which has all the supreme virtues that every nation arrogates to itself. That one is the one to which my reader belongs." And I got a letter from a Pole saying, "I'm so glad you recognize the superiority of Poland."
> [Bertrand Russell Speaks his Mind. New York: The World Publishing Company 1960: 101.]

Bertrand Russell's anecdote would be equally credible had the subject matter of his discussion been the national language rather than the nation, languages being as they are the most powerful symbolic vehicles of nationalism. Russell's message is unmistakable: Nationalism is an attitude which is irreconcilable with rational behavior.

In this book no judgments are passed about the merits or dangers of the political instrumentalization of language. Rather, an attempt is made to shed some light on the notion of 'national language' from various angles in order to understand what it is all about. More than 4000 languages are spoken on this planet, but only a small minority of them have a reasonable claim to being called *national languages*. How do they differ from others that are not national languages? Are there any linguistic features that distinguish national languages from others, or is the difference a purely political one? What are the conditions for a language to become a national language? What functions must such a language be able to fulfil? And do national languages fulfil similar functions in different societies? Those are some of the questions raised in this book. Rather than discussing them in the abstract, however, they are addressed here with respect to particular examples of various languages in different parts of the world. A differentiated answer to the general question forming the title of this book thus becomes possible.

The issues addressed in this book were first discussed at a workshop which I had the privilege to organize at Georgetown University on the occasion of the 1985 LSA Institute. Preliminary versions of some of the chapters of this book were presented at the workshop, others were solicited later. The entrance of the auditorium in which the workshop took place is marked with a motto by Teilhard de Chardin: "The age of nations is past . . . " The chapters of this book combine to show, each one from its own viewpoint, that this is a rather wishful claim. In the age of superpowers the nation is as important a form of social organization as ever, and the notion of national language continues to be both meaningful and a crucial catalyst for political attitudes and movements.

F. C.
Washington, D.C.
December 1986

What is a National Language Good for?

Florian Coulmas

The question 'What is a national language good for?' is a historical question in a twofold sense: It is an old question that has been asked before many times, and answered, and it is a question every answer to which is historically conditioned. The gist of the question and the validity of every given answer depend on the historical circumstances. It is useful, therefore, to reconsider 'the national language question'[1] from time to time.

Shortly after World War II, Otto Jespersen wrote the following:

> The greatest and most important phenomenon of the evolution of language in historic times has been the springing up of the great national common languages . . . which have driven out, or are on the way to drive out, the local dialects purely conditioned by geographical factors (Jespersen 1946: 39).

This statement seems to imply that there is something special about national languages that distinguishes them from others that are not national languages. Obviously, there are functional differences. Only some languages are **national languages**. The world is divided at present into some 160 states most of which have explicitly or implicitly designated one language as their national

1

language. This means that there are about thirty to forty times as many languages as national languages. What are the few good for, and how do they differ from the many?

Jespersen's statement suggests that the 'national common languages'—to him basically the big European standard languages associated with a given nation state—came into a position of dominance 'purely conditioned by *geographical* factors.' This is misleading. While geographical contingencies have played an undeniable role in the linguistic development of Europe, socio-historical and ideological factors were much more important. The question is how language could grow into such a powerful political symbol that it came to be seen as a sign of loyalty; that its use was, at times, outlawed or punished like that of Catalonian in Spain or that of other languages than French in post-revolutionary France (cf. Jacob and Gordon 1985); that people would kill each other or burn themselves in the street for the sake of their language, as Tamils have been reported to do in newly independent India and nowadays in Sri Lanka (cf. Hellmann-Rajanayagam 1983, Jupp 1978); that anybody even cares to listen to war cries for 'the defense of **our** language,' such as have been published recently by U.S. English,[2] a xenophobic language movement in the United States. Why, on the other hand, is Switzerland invariably cited as the odd exception (e.g. Haugen 1985) of a country where linguistic pluralism is not disruptive for the nation, or rather where the development of nationhood overcame the diversity of tongues? Why, indeed, should the peaceful coexistence of several languages within one country not always be considered a desirable goal?

The fact of the matter is that many people, especially in the Western world, nowadays take it for granted that there is a providential bond between language and nation: The idea of a natural unity of nation, state, and language has proved to be one of the most successful pieces of Western political ideology since the French Revolution. In the nineteenth century language became the most powerful symbol of nationalism. As Deutsch (1942) pointed out, between 1800 and 1900, the number of fullfledged national languages in Europe doubled.[3] The underlying force, which Toynbee (1965: 247) calls 'the evil spirit of *Linguistic Nationalism*,' eventually disrupted the outmoded multilingual empire of the Hapsburg Monarchy, as ever more language groups (re-)discovered and claimed their identity and political autonomy with it.

This was nationalism in the technical sense in which it is usually understood today, that is, a force that created unity across societal strata, whose coming into existence was thus intimately related to the transformation of feudal into bourgeois societies which, in turn, depended on the expansion of secular education in the vernacular languages (cf. Emerson 1960: 147). This historical scheme is often applied in explaining the nexus of language and nationalism. As the nation state is a political concept whose full vigor emerged only in response to the Napoleonic wars, the national language ideology is also often characterized as an outgrowth of the French Revolution. 'Nationalism,' writes Minogue (1967: 33) 'is a European invention.'

Especially the Romantic movement is regularly credited, or blamed, for popularizing the national language issue and elevating language to become one of the prime paraphernalia of a nation. Herder is persistently cited in this connection (cf. e. g. Barnard 1965, Minogue 1967, Fishman 1972, Smith 1981, Edwards 1985). His influence was undeniably significant in his time and throughout the 19th century. However, while he may have been the most eloquent and passionate defender of his mother tongue as a national asset, he was by no means the first to address the topic.

From Enlightenment to Romanticism

A hundred years before Herder, Leibniz made a plea for the German language that already contained all of the important arguments concerning language, education, societal welfare, and national unity. Like all of his fellow intellectuals, Leibniz wrote almost exclusively in French and Latin, yet, in his Admonition to the Germans of 1683, he stated that 'it is found in all history that usually nation and language flourish together.' 'Taking on a foreign language,' on the other hand, 'has normally brought with it loss of freedom and a foreign yoke' (Leibniz 1697).

When Leibniz wrote, there were good reasons to be concerned about the fate of the German language. Socially stratifying bilingualism was widespread, establishing an effective barrier between the nobility who conversed among themselves in French, and the common people who spoke German. Also, the Thirty Years War had left Germany devastated, while other European countries, Louis XIV's France in particular, enjoyed a period of great cultural achievement. Political and religious unity in Germany was destroyed; there was no political or cultural center. Germany was reduced to a developing country. Her intellectual and power élites were attracted by the glamour of their more advanced neighbors, and, instead of cultivating German, they used French for all purposes of higher communication.

Although Leibniz, who was a member of the Académie Française and of the Royal Society, also did just that, he realized the political implications of the neglect of the German language by the élites. It is perhaps because he held office as a high-ranking counsellor at the Court of Hanover for several decades that he had a sense of the political dimensions of language choice. While he diagnosed 'a deficit in our language,' especially in expressions 'referring to morality, passion of the mind, social intercourse, governmental matters, and all sorts of affairs of civil and public life' (1697) he also saw very clearly 'that the Germans do not lack the ability, but the resolution to elevate their language throughout' (ibid.). French was not being used because the German language was inadequate. Rather it was the other way round: German had failed to develop and adapt to the purposes of modern communication because the élites, out of snobbery, had neglected it preferring to speak French. The problem, therefore, was to motivate the nobility and the intellectuals to speak and write German instead of French (and Latin).

This was not easy, because the upper classes had little to gain from using boorish German instead of elegant French. In the contrary, they would give up a powerful means of defending their privileges. Language was very efficiently employed as a marker of social distinction rather than unity. In order to promote the vernacular, Leibniz therefore had to persuade the élites that they, too, would benefit from the cultivation of German.

His arguments reflect the fact that he was a patriot and believed in enlightenment. 'The more such [educated] people there are in a country,' he wrote, 'the more refined and civilized the nation, and the happier and braver its inhabitants' (Leibniz 1683). Leibniz thus highlighted the **nation** as the superordinate concern. He spoke of 'a service to the fatherland,' and contrasted the poor state of the German language in which only 'few straightforward books are written . . . that have the right taste or savor' with that of Italian, French, and English where 'the splendor of wisdom is not reserved to the learned men only but has trickled down to the mother tongue' (ibid.). Scholarly writing in the language of the people was a prerequisite of spreading education in society, and that, Leibniz argued, was for the glory and benefit of the nation. If Germany wanted to compete with her neighbors, education in the vernacular was essential. And in order to make this possible, the vernacular needed to be upgraded and refined.

Leibniz may have believed in both enlightenment and language cultivation as values in their own right, but he knew that these lofty ideals were hardly convincing enough for recruiting the élites' active support for the vernacular. Therefore, he emphasized the nation as a social bond and the significance of a cultivated language and more widely spread education for its welfare and glory. He proposed the establishment of a German-minded Society [*Deutschgesinnte Gesellschaft*] and became involved in founding the Prussian Academy of Science whose constitution he wrote. Furthermore, he prescribed a number of specific measures designed as a therapy for the ailing German language, such as systematic vocabulary enrichenment by recycling old words that had fallen out of use, terminology formation by drawing on native German stock, and abolishing unnecessary German words. And he strongly criticized those of his contemporaries who neglected the German language while failing to learn French properly.

It is important to note, however, that Leibniz' recommendations bore the mark of true enlightenment. Promoting the national language for him meant neither narrow-minded purism nor hostility toward other nations. He explicitly stated that he 'was not of the opinion that one ought to become a puritan in language and, for superstitious fear, avoid a foreign but handy word as a mortal sin, thus debilitating oneself and depriving one's words of emphasis' (Leibniz 1683). For the cosmopolitan Leibniz, the notion of national language was a vehicle of enlightenment. The shriller tones of nationalism were only later to accompany, if not drown, the theme of 'one language, one nation, one state'.

However, already in the early eighteenth century, Leibniz' followers, the grammarians and lexicographers who took it upon themselves to provide the technical means of cultivating the German language that Leibniz had demanded, turned his rational concern about the decline of German into provincial pedantry. Gottsched devoted his life to writing a grammar of German as a national task. In the preface to its second edition of 1749 he took the fact that the first had sold well as an indication of patriotism (Gottsched 1749). Part of the rationale for writing a German grammar was to demonstrate to the world that the Germans had just as good and regular a language as any of their neighbors.

Another theme that Leibniz introduced into the discussion about upgrading the German language on entirely rational grounds, but which later was to receive a different ideological coating, concerns foreign words and terminology. Leibniz had observed that technical terms [*Kunstwörter*] made up of German morphemes were easier to understand for people with no formal education in Latin schools than Latin or Greek loan-words. As he saw it, loanwords and foreign words did not have to be avoided at all cost, but, then, they also should not be used where native words were readily available. Rather than adopting such a pragmatic attitude, lexicographers like Adelung and Campe began the tradition—still prevailing in German lexicography—of distinguishing the genuinely German from foreign parts of the vocabulary and, sometimes absurdly, coining native alternatives for non-German words.

The rationalization provided for this approach was based on a deterministic view of the relation between language and conceptualization: The lexicon of a language incorporated a particular vision of the world (which should not be contaminated by foreign elements). Klopstock, for instance, a poet who also theorized about principles of writing a new German grammar and dictionary, expressed this idea very clearly. In his polemical essay *Die deutsche Gelehrtenrepublik* he wrote that 'every language is, as it were, a repository of the most characteristic notions of a nation' (1774/1975: 120). In the Romantic movement, this idea should be fully exploited for the purposes of nationalistic mysticism.

Leibniz had a deep interest in the diversity of languages which was, however, counterbalanced by his interest in universality. Also, as far as language use was concerned, his view was basically instrumental: Cultivating German was desirable in the best interest of spreading general education. For the Romanticists, on the other hand, cultivating German was desirable because the German language enshrined the spirit of the German nation. Leibniz, too, saw an intimate connection between language and thought. Language for him was 'like a mirror of the mind' (1683). But as such it was also an instrument of rational thinking.

Fichte, by contrast, like Leibniz an eminent philosopher who advocated philanthropic devotion to knowledge as a national goal, was much less sober in his ideas concerning language and the German language in particular. He build his theoretical scaffold on the idea that a **living** language expresses the soul of a nation. Like Klopstock, Herder, and others, he believed in determinism: The way a nation thinks and conceptualizes the world depends on its language. In his *Addresses to the German Nation*, which were written and delivered during the crisis of Napoleon's invasions and French occupation, Fichte stated that 'those who speak the same language are linked together, before human intervention takes a hand, by mere nature through a host of invisible ties . . . they are by nature one indivisible whole.' Thus, 'wherever a distinct language is found, there also exists a distinct nation' (Fichte 1808). In his political thinking the nation became a historical subject and the language its voice.

The idea that language somehow incorporates the soul of a nation was not the product of Fichte's mind. However, he did not stop there. He also theorized about qualitative differences between languages. His arguments about language and 'its immeasurable influence on the entire human development of a nation' (ibid.) must be read as the thoughts of an ardent nationalist who realized that under conditions of foreign domination and political fragmentation the language was virtually the only culture marker that could serve as a common bond and symbol of the nation. It was important, therefore, to set this language apart from others. Because of the élites' preference for French[4] German had a reputation of being less classy and elegant. In this respect German differed most obviously from the language of the hated Western neighbors. The problem was how this difference, which for Germans was hard to be proud of, could be exploited for nationalistic purposes. Fichte's solution was the rather stunning distinction he drew between 'living' and 'dead' languages. 'A living language,' he wrote, 'if compared with another one, can well be highly cultivated, but it can never in itself achieve the same perfection and formation that a dead language so easily obtains' (Fichte 1808).

The distinction between living and dead languages is stunning, because by the latter Fichte did not mean Hebrew, Greek, and Latin only, but French, Italian, and English as well. Living languages were those with an unbroken and 'pure' tradition, such as German. Dead languages, on the other hand, were languages with mixed and broken-off traditions like Latin-Celtic French or English, for that matter. French had cut off its Latin roots by becoming a language in its own right; and English, since the Norman conquest, was a mixed language altogether, whereas German constituted a continuous link with the past from time immemorial. It could not be bent and polished at will because, unlike the dead languages, it had a character. Such ideological acrobatics allowed Fichte to turn a vice into a virtue: German was not only distinct from other languages, but alive and more authentic than others incorporating, as it did, the spirit of the *Urvolk*. The Germans, he said, speak 'a language which is shaped to express the truth' (ibid.).

Fichte not only established a rightful place for the German language in the German society, but his extravagant distinction between 'living' and 'dead' languages allowed him to single it out as a special language. It was this irrational part of his argument that proved attractive and versatile because any speech community could adapt it for its purposes.[5] Language, so the argument goes, is a traditional bond, a kind of emotional community because it defines a conceptualization of the world that is genuinely that of its nation. It rests on and guarantees the continuation of a tradition.

Using a foreign language, therefore, means to cut off one's roots and surrender one's conceptualization of the world to that of the foreign speech community. It is, indeed, as Klopstock (1774) put it, nothing short of treason.

The idea of the individuality of each different language as a peculiar property of the nation who speaks it was most subtly and theoretically viably elaborated by Wilhelm von Humboldt. A key notion in his linguistic thinking is that of **the character of languages**,[6] some essential quality of every language which remains hard to grasp no matter how much one analyzes and describes it, since it is a product of its own past. This is clearly reminiscent of Fichte, and the same **Zeitgeist** no doubt emanates from their work. Yet, Humboldt reduced the question of the differences between languages and their relationship with nations to systematic investigation. He carried further Herder's notion of the inseparability of language and thought; and thus also came to the conclusion that differences between languages involve differences in the understanding and interpretation of the world.

Language for Humboldt was essentially a social phenomenon, that is, an achievement that unites individuals while separating groups. These groups are nations; and they cannot be thought of without language and vice versa, since 'our historiography nowhere justifies the assumption that a nation ever existed prior to its language, or, to put it differently, that a language was ever formed solely by the nation to which it belongs' (Humboldt 1823/1963: 69). Hence, 'the concept of a nation must be based especially upon language' (1830/1963: 561). 'Language by its own force proclaims the national character' (ibid.).

Humboldt's thinking was primarily historical rather than political and so was his concern with the relationship between language and nation. However, the fact that his reasoning was quite detached from political affairs then current made it a particularly attractive point of reference for every nationalist who wanted to exploit language for his purposes. Humboldt argued that 'the concept of the nation as a host of people constructing a language in a definite manner is directly manifest through language' (ibid.). In principle, this argumentation could be adapted by anyone who wanted to use language for claiming nationhood and fuelling nationalist movements. Which was, in fact, what many nineteenth century nationalists especially in Eastern and Northern Europe and on the Balkan peninsula did (cf. Smith 1981: 46).

Industrialization, urbanization, and growing linguistic nationalism in Western Europe influenced the crystallization of ethnic and linguistic identities elsewhere on the continent. Finland is a good example. Until the nineteenth century, Finnish was basically a spoken language. It emerged very suddenly as a symbol of national identity. The first political parties in Finland were language parties, which came into existence in the middle of the nineteenth century. The point at issue was the traditional Swedish-Finnish bilingualism where Swedish figured as the minority élite language. The speed with which Finnish developed into the dominant language as a result of the nationalist movement is quite remarkable, and so is the relatively little amount of hardship and resentment it produced on the part of the Swedish minority (cf. Allpuro 1976). Estonian, Serbo-Croatian, and Albanian are other examples of languages that became symbols of national movements and developed their modern standard form only in the nineteenth century (cf. Haarmann 1975, chp. 3).

Other languages, such as, French, English, Dutch, Danish, Russian, and Swedish were, however, well-established as national languages before the surge of nationalism in the nineteenth century. Yet, while the nexus of language and nation had been invoked much earlier, it was put into a consistent ideological context and provided with some scientific underpinning during the Romantic period. It was a reaction partly to the French Revolution one of whose aims it was to impose a central national language on all the people of France, and partly to the Napoleonic wars that stimulated a sense of anti-French and anti-foreign sentiment, pride, and demand for autonomy all over Europe. Language had become the most prominent symbol of nationhood which had consequences for both the internal and external organization of political entities.

Language, nation, and state

Stressing the identity of language and nation is one thing, but demanding political autonomy for a linguistically defined group is, of course, something quite different. Languages have always been used to establish or claim a sphere of influence. As imperial languages they have been imposed on dominated ethnic groups by whoever had the power to do so. A uniform code has more often than not been regarded as a matter of administrative convenience for governing a country or empire. However, ideologizing language is a different matter; and if language can be employed as a symbol of national unity by a dominant group, dominated groups may, of course, exert the same logic and make political claims based on their linguistic identity. Thus, while the idea of a national language and its political enforcement may be said to function as a cohesive force, the reverse is also true. Language may be as disruptive a force as any culture marker, and it is clear that the national language-ideology has bred intra-communal strife and, in a sense, created minorities in many countries that have established themselves as states in modern times.

The Greek language movement during the closing decades of the eighteenth century, for instance, played an essential role in the Greeks' struggle against Turkish rule.[7] As the question of the establishment of a modern nation state became the order of the day, the need for modernizing and standardizing Greek as a genuine national language came to be felt and discussed. Adamantios Korais, a patriot and scholar and the most influential figure in the language movement, wanted to purify Greek from Turkish loan-words as well as from aberrant dialect features in phonology, morphology, and syntax. His ideal was to create a language capable of expressing everything and understood by all. Only such a language was suitable for the education and intellectual liberation of the people. This purified Greek was to be the vehicle of education in the free Greece to come and for the expression of the Greek spirit.

Eventually the Greek nationalists succeeded in shaking off the foreign yoke and seceded from the moribund multilingual Ottoman empire. Korais' peculiarly archaising *katharevousa* [pure language] was established as the national tongue of the new Greek state. This was a fine solution for the majority, at least as far as their nationalist needs were concerned.[8] But then, new minorities came into existence in the Greek nation state as a byproduct, as it were, of this policy: Turks, Macedonians, Albanians, and Rumanians.

The establishment of the *katharevousa* as the language of the modern Greek nation state is only one example of many that could be presented to illustrate the fact that the politicization of language, while helping one group to achieve its goals, is likely to create new problems for others. Multilingualism is a pervasive, not a marginal phenomenon. The real question about the national language idea is therefore whether language can be politically instrumentalized without becoming a means of suppression and making it ever more difficult for different language groups to live together peacefully. Haugen (1985: 5) observed that 'it would actually be hard to point out a single European nation that does not have a minority problem, in the sense of having within its borders a population speaking some language that cannot be regarded as just a dialect of the national tongue.'

This is undoubtedly true. The monolingual state and, by consequence, the true nation state, has always been the odd exception rather than the rule.[9] It is by no means self-evident, therefore, why linguistic pluralism is generally regarded as a problem. Beer (1985: 216) has noted that language differences within a polity do not in themselves lead to disruption of national unity. That language movements come into existence, that language becomes a political instrument whose employment actually leaves traces on the political map does not happen often. Weinstein has asserted that political movements centered upon a language can affect frontiers 'only during key moments in the history of the rise of ethnic and national groupings' (Weinstein 1979: 362). What are these key moments, that is, under what circumstances does language become a catalyst of political forces?

In Europe where the nation state as a form of political organization originated, and where most of the great standard languages radiated from a political or cultural center being superposed on other closely related dialects, the national language-ideology had some credibility. The linguistic criterion was of great importance, indeed, in the European context, in marking one nation from another. In Kedourie's influential theory of nationalism, language figures as the major defining feature: 'A group speaking the same language is known as a nation, and a nation ought to constitute a state' (1961: 68). Since the beginning of the nineteenth century, this belief had many adherents in Europe. Moreover, the gradual spread of print culture and general education helped to convince people that the identity of language, nation, and state is a natural and hence desirable principle of organizing the world. However, the notion that each nation is, or should be, endowed with a language of its own, comes into serious conflict with demographic and political realities when applied to other parts of the world, Asia, Africa, and the Pacific in particular. While this should be obvious in view of the great diversity of languages in these areas, the national language-ideology was embraced by nationalists there, too. Several different political issues are involved here, and they interfere with each other.

First of all, the national language question in Asia and sub-Saharan Africa is a question of post-colonial history. That means, briefly, that the slogan 'one language, one nation, one state' has to be worked backwards. Decolonization produced new states, but not necessarily new nations, let alone new national languages. The new states bear the stamp of the colonial legacy, as their boundaries more often than not reflect power relations between the European colonizers rather than ethnic or historical realities in the colonized territories. Thus, while the nation state in Europe was largely a product of the nation whose awakening sense of identity called for the establishment of a politically autonomous organization; in the new polities of the post-colonial epoch, this has to be produced by a state, which exists as an institutional structure without a nation that pays loyalty to it. In this context, language did not easily offer itself as a cohesive symbol. Smith (1971) has pointed out that, in Africa, nationalism is rarely centered upon language since this could lead to 'balkanisation.' As a matter of fact, after independence, many Third World countries have avoided the language issue because of its explosive potential. However, attempts at raising the educational level of the population at large, especially literacy campaigns in rural areas, made policy discussions, and decisions about language eventually inevitable. Thus, in multilingual countries, functional considerations such as the desire to have an administrative language for the whole country and the belief that primary education is more effective if provided in the students' mother tongues came into conflict with each other. And although most Third World countries have many other pressing priorities, they could eventually not ignore the symbolic aspects of the national language question and their importance for the process of nation-building. A brief look at the linguistic heritage of colonialism may clarify this point.

One of the most remarkable characteristics and lasting effects of imperialism was that European languages were superimposed on the native languages of the colonized peoples. This happened partly as a matter of administrative convenience without much ideological zeal, and partly as a matter of fulfilling a 'civilizing mission.'[10] The British and the Dutch exemplify the first instance. They did not really care whether English and Dutch were spread widely in their colonies. To the contrary, it was the leaders of the colonized people who demanded instruction in these languages in order to get access to better education (cf. Panikkar 1969: 246; Alisjahbana 1984: 80) while the British and Dutch colonizers long preferred to administer their colonies through coopted local élites in their own local languages. The Portuguese and the French exemplify the second instance pursuing, as they did, a policy of active suppression of local languages in their colonies, *linguistic genocide* as Haugen (1973) calls it. Calvet (1974: 68) cites the duc de Rovigo's unmistakable statement of the aims of the French education policy in Algeria in the early phase of colonization in 1832:

> Je regard la propagation de l'instruction et de notre langue comme le moyen le plus efficace de faire de progrès à notre domination dans ce pays . . . Le vrai prodige à opérer serait de remplacer peu à peu l'arabe par le français.

While the French were more blunt than the British in their linguistic imperialism, they were not more successful. Indeed, the spread of English is by far the most striking example of language expansion in all recorded history. I believe that this is due partly to a snowball effect and partly to the fact that English underwent relatively early a process of denationalization. When the British colonies in North America became independent, the newly emerging nation, with the help of nationalists like Noah Webster and others, also shook off the British standard for the English language, elevating what was until then a regional and basically sub-standard variety to a standard in its own right. The American example and the fact that the spread of English was never an important issue of Britain's colonial policy made it easier for former colonies to retain English after independence. Yet, the ideological problems of post-colonial language policy were, and, to some extent, still are considerable.

Even though the British were rather low-key as regards the symbolic value they attached to English in the handling of their colonial affairs, the use of English became a symbol of colonialism just as French, Dutch, or any other imperial language. What Gandhi wrote about the native Indian languages and about English before independence leaves no doubt about it. As early as 1909 Gandhi subscribed publicly to linguistic nationalism when he wrote that it 'would be no exaggeration to say that those who give up their language are traitors to their country and people' (Gandhi 1965: 2). Instead of simply arguing against the use of English by Indians for practical reasons and calling for cultivating the native languages, he adopted the national language-ideology and in 1917 stated that 'Hindi[11] alone can become the national language' (Gandhi 1965: 11). He spoke of the *national necessity* to learn Hindi in non-Hindi speaking parts of India (ibid. 20). Indeed, to establish Hindi as the national language of India was one of the dominant themes of the independence movement, and the symbolic value of the language question was highlighted by the Indians rather than the British, as in Gandhi's article of 1946. 'People seem to be drunk with the wine of English and they speak English in their clubs, in their home and everywhere. *They are denationalized*' (Gandhi 1965: 93, emph. added). After independence had been achieved, Gandhi continued to fight the use of English: 'My plea is for banishing English as a cultural usurper as we successfully banished the political rule of the English usurper' (ibid. 116).

There were, of course, other politicians in India as well as in other former colonies who stressed the practical advantages of the colonial languages for governing their newly independent countries. As languages of higher education, commerce, and international communication, they were an important link with the outside world providing access to the scientific literature of the West and, this was the expectation, to the development that goes with it.

Also, the somewhat paradoxical function the colonial languages played for independence movements did not go unnoticed. All of what Gandhi wrote about English was, after all, written in English. Thus Ayyangar, an active participant of the Indian independence movement, agues with some justification that 'English was the language on which we have built and achieved our freedom' (Srivastava 1979: 85). Many Indians still believe that the English language rather than Hindi provided them with a common means of nation-wide communication and evocation of their inherent feeling of 'Indian-ness' (Le Page 1964: 60). The spread of Hindi, on the other hand, was interpreted, especially in the Dravidian states of the south, 'as Hinduisation[12] rather than Indianisation' (Pattanayak 1985: 405). It is not surprising, therefore, that the policy of replacing English by Hindi within 15 years after independence failed and had to be supplanted by the potentially indefinite recognition of English as India's co-official language.

The Indian situation epitomizes the dilemma of the national language question in post-colonial states. The superposed European language was a medium of creating a feeling of togetherness and a vital instrument of the independence struggle. Yet, it spells one's own inadequacy in the face of foreign dominance and is such a visible remnant of colonialism that many oppose it as a symbol of neo-colonialism.

In many of the inheritor states there is, however, no obvious alternative. Changing the administrative language of a country is not only a matter of linguistic adequacy, that is, of having a language sufficiently standardized and equipped with the technical terminology necessary for advanced forms of communication in government, science, technology, and education, and accepted by all parts of the population. It also involves enormous economic costs that have been prohibitive for many post-colonial countries. Not surprisingly, the cases where the colonial language was effectively replaced by a home-grown language after independence are very rare indeed. The replacement of Dutch by Bahasa Indonesia was greatly aided by the Japanese occupation of Indonesia in 1942. Dutch was banned by the occupational forces practically overnight; and, because Japanese could not be implemented rapidly as administrative language, the Bahasa Indonesia movement was greatly boosted, gaining enough momentum to successfully continue the nation-wide spread of this variety of Malay as Indonesia's national language after independence (cf. Alisjahbana 1971, Lowenberg in this volume). Similarly favorable conditions obtained in Tanzania where Swahili had been used for centuries as a regional lingua franca and thus could compete with English since it had a written history and was accepted widely by the population. For the rest, the colonial languages have survived decolonization almost everywhere. Attempts to replace them were either avoided, as in most Black African countries, or met with little success, as in the Maghreb where French thrives more than ever in spite of vigorous Arabization programs.

Replacing the colonial language by an autochthonous one is, however, not the only solution for the embarrassing language issue in the Third World. Proponents of the colonial languages in the inheritor countries have found another interesting way out of the dilemma seemingly satisfying nationalist sentiments as well as practical concerns of education and development that allows them to take advantage of the inescapable forces history exercises on language. English will remain in India, writes Pattanayak, a native of Oriya, 'because it has become part of the Indian heritage' (op. cit. 406). *Heritage*, of course, is one of the central themes of nationalist reasoning; and English has, of course, become part of the Indian heritage in a more than symbolic sense. Many politicians, scholars, and writers in West Africa make exactly the same point about French. The language of liberation movements in French colonies was French; and *francophonie* still has an enormous appeal for the African élites who, like Léopold Senghor (1956) subscribe to the idea, 'don't deny your past, make it part of yourself!' A possible answer to the national language ideology of the West and its neo-colonial implications is thus to turn the once prototypical national languages that the European colonial powers spread all over the globe into transnational languages that are no longer any particular nation's property.

Two conflicting tendencies are at work here that are much more obvious and further advanced in English than in French. On the one hand, the practical advantages of the former colonial languages are seen in their having developed into *international* languages; while on the other hand, they acquire new varieties, giving expression to *national* identities. Indian English, Jamaican English, Philippine English, Singapore English, Nigerian English, etc. have become firmly established on the linguistic map of the world;[13] and like American English they are moving in the direction of becoming a powerful symbol of national identity, which in multilingual and multicultural countries such as India or the countries of Black Africa none of the native languages could ever be.

By interpreting 'localized forms of English' (Strevens 1983) as national characteristics and making them part of a national heritage, the practical consideration that, with a national language, it is easier to develop the institutional infrastructure of a polity is provided with some ideological suprastructure. What Kelman (1971) calls the instrumental attachment to a national system is gradually supplemented with a sentimental attachment.

This process of re-nationalizing the former colonial transnational languages of wider communication once again demonstrates the force of the national language ideology. Why, one might want to ask, have the multilingual countries of Asia and Africa played the national language theme at all? Why is it that a common language is generally seen as such an important ingredient of nation-building? Why are the symbolic values of a national language highlighted in the face of the enormous lack of coincidence between language, nation, and state in most parts of the world? Where linguistic diversity exists, the effort to establish a national language with ideological zeal is bound to generate conflict. Why, then, is not the multiplicity of languages of a given country stressed as a matter of pride, while the language for communicating on the national level is restricted to a practical convenience without any sentimental value? That a community's sense of identity is bound up with its language seems obvious enough; for a common language secures mutual understanding while at the same time being a link with the past. However, if the concept of a nation has anything at all to do with language, as most theoreticians on this issue have taken for granted, then the nation state is hardly a very natural unit of identification in most parts of the world.

One of the most surprising facts about the post-colonial epoch

is that virtually all of the established political frontiers have remained intact and almost none of the inheritor states have fallen
apart.[14] For lack of any other political philosophy, the mostly
European educated leaders of the post-colonial societies have
adopted the assumption that there is a natural division of human-
ity into nations and that the nation state is the natural and ultimate
form of political organization. They have thus embarked on the
enterprise of nation building. The essence of nation building is the
search for collective identity which the leaders of the inheritor
states have by and large recognized as a value in its own right.
With it they accepted the dogma of Renaissance nationalism which
had assigned language such a prominent role. Ideologically the
quest for a national language in Third World countries can be
interpreted as a response to the existence of national languages in
Europe and their symbolic significance for national integrity. Just
as there is no room for a political vacuum in the modern world
which is almost completely cut up into more or less autonomous
states, it seems to be impossible to dispense with the idea of a
national language.

The historical relationships between language, nation, and
state are, however, incomparable in the countries of Western
Europe and their former colonies. The leaders of the new states
believe that the business of nation building cannot be accomplished without a national language. Thus the state puts much
emphasis on the spread of a common language in order to inspire a
sense of national identity. In the European context, a sense of
national identity and its association with a language existed prior
to the modern state.

Assessing the national language ideology today, we find that
this piece of political philosophy which originated in the Renaissance and came to full bloom together with Romantic nationalism
has not lost its force. It still fuels debate and controversy in many
parts of the world, East and West, North and South. New languages keep emerging as potential national languages and are
turned into vehicles of political claims by their promoters, as, for
instance Punjabi in India. At the same time, the classical national
languages are coming under pressure as more and more population shifts are taking place which magnify linguistic and ethnic

diversity in the consolidated nation states. So far, Third World countries have failed to put forth an attractive alternative ideology that combines linguistic pluralism with nationalism. The former colonial powers, on the other hand, while willy-nilly making some allowances for minorities, show no inclination to discard the national language ideology. Thus, in spite of the 'new ethnicity' and an increasing awareness of linguistic pluralism almost everywhere, on the one hand, and, on the other hand, the ever growing importance of English, the world language of our time, for transnational communication, the national language question, unmodern as it may seem, is not yet obsolete.

Notes

1. The title of Le Page's 1964 book.
2. For a critical assessment see Donahue 1985.
3. Cf. also Kloss 1952.
4. As late as 1750, Voltaire could write home from Potsdam, *"L' allemand est pour les soldats et pour les chevaux."* Since the French revolution the situation had somewhat improved—after all, Lessing and Wieland, Goethe and Schiller had published their great works in the meantime—but the scars of the social stigmatization of the German language were not yet completely healed at the turn of the century.
5. Notice, for example, how Kindaichi, a leading Japanese linguist, according to Miller presents essentially the same argument:

> Japanese is "truly and lamentably poor, weak, and deficient in this or that quality or element. But lo and behold! We are still very fortunate to have this language, and . . . I will be able to demonstrate how this defect really works to our advantage. Finally, a genial coda is appended to each of these praise-for-blame transformations to the effect that if you want to see a language that is really defective, you should take a look at Chinese or Korean, both of which Kindaichi categorizes as being 'sick languages'. Japanese, it goes without saying, is a healthy language" (Miller 1982: 120).

6. Cf. Wilhelm von Humboldt (1830–1835).
7. Cf. Caratzas 1958, Browning 1969.
8. In other respects the establishment of *katharevousa* as the language of the state, which it was until 1976, was not such a happy language policy. By this measure the standardization of the vernacular was delayed, and a situation of great dialect variety transformed into institutionalized diglossia. Cf. Alexiou 1982.

9. Connor (1978) found that only 9.1 per cent of all states were true nation states in the sense of a polity comprising a homogeneous national group. 37.9 per cent were states dominated by a major ethnic group comprising more than three-quarters of the total population. 23.5 per cent had ethnic majorities ranging between half and three-quarters of the population, and in the remaining 29.5 per cent of all states the largest ethnic group accounted for less than half of the population.

10. For a fuller discussion of the differences between the British policy of *indirect rule* and the French colonial concept of *assimilation* see Spencer 1974; Coulmas 1985, chapter 4.

11. At that time, Gandhi was not yet completely consistent in his terminology using both *Hindi* and *Hindustani*. This is an important difference since *Hindi* implies Sanskritisation which is unacceptable to the Muslim population. *Hindustani*, by contrast, a variety that had evolved out of contact between Hindi and Urdu speakers in the bazaars and barracks, was seen by Gandhi as having an integrative potential. In his later writings he was careful usually to make a clear distinction between the two. It was Hindustani what he promoted rather than Hindi.

12. This should not be taken to have any religious implications, after all, the southern Indians are Hindus. What Pattanayak means by "Hinduisation" is "domination of the South by the North."

13. This development has attracted much attention lately. *English* has acquired a plural form not only in the title of books (e.g. Platt, Weber, Ho 1984), but a scientific journal, *World Englishes*, has been founded whose declared purpose is to study "English as an international and intranational language."

14. Bangladesh is, of course, an important exception. What it illustrates, most importantly in the present context, is that markers of national identity and allegiance are variable. The same Bengali people who stressed their religious identity in order to create the new state of Pakistan while downplaying the Bengali language as a common bond with their Hindu brethren in 1947, chose to assert their linguistic identity in breaking away from Pakistan and creating the independent state of Bangladesh in 1971 (cf. Das Gupta 1985).

References

Alexiou, Margaret. 1982. Diglossia in Greece. In: W. Haas, ed. *Standard Languages, Spoken and Written.*Manchester: Manchester University Press, 156–192.

Alisjahbana, S. Takdir. 1971. Language Policy, Language Engeneering and Literacy in Indonesia and Malaysia. In: T. Sebeok, ed. *Current Trends in Linguistics* 8. The Hague: Mouton, 1025–1038.

Alisjahbana, S. Takdir. 1984. The Concept of Language Standardisation and its Application to the Indonesian Language. In: F. Coulmas, ed. *Linguistic Minorities and Literacy*. Berlin, New York, Amsterdam: Mouton, 77–98.

Allapuro, Risto. 1976. Nineteenth-Century Nationalism in Finland: A Comparative Perspective. *Scandinavian Political Studies* 2. A9–29.

Barnard, F. M. 1965. *Herder's Social and Political Thought: From Enlightenment to Nationalism.* Oxford: Clarendon Press.

Beer, W. R. 1985. Toward a Theory of Linguistic Mobilization. In: W.R.Beer and J.E. Jacob, eds. *Language Policy and National Unity.* Totowa, N.J.: Rowman&Allanheld,217–235.

Browning, Robert. 1969. *Medieval and Modern Greek.* London: Hutchinson University Library.

Calvet, Louis-Jean. 1974. *Linguistique et colonialisme, petit traitè de glottophagie.* Paris: Edition Payot.

Caratzas, S. C. 1958. Die Entstehung der neugriechischen Literatursprache. *Glotta* 36: 194–208.

Connor, W. 1978. A Nation is a Nation, is a State, is an Ethnic Group, is a . . . *Ethnic and Racial Studies* 3, 355–59.

Coulmas, Florian. 1985. *Sprache und Staat. Studien zu Sprachplanung und Sprachpolitik.* Berlin, New York: De Gruyter.

Das Guptas, Jyotirindra. 1985. Language, National Unity, and Shared Development in South Asia. In: W.R. Beer and J.E. Jacob, eds. *Language Policy and National Unity.* Totowa, N.J.: Rowman & Allanheld, 198–216.

Deutsch, Karl W. 1942. The Trend of European Nationalism. *American Political Science Review* 36: 533–541.

Donahue, Thomas S. 1985. 'U.S. English': Its Life and Works. *International Journal of the Sociology of Language* 56: 99- 112.

Edwards, John. 1985. *Language, Society and Identity.* New York: Blackwell.

Emerson, Rupert. 1960. *From Empire to Nation. The Rise to Self- Assertion of Asian and African Peoples.* Boston: Beacon Press.

Fichte, Johann Gottlieb. 1808. Reden an die deutsche Nation In: *Sämtliche Werke*, I.H. Fichte, ed. 8 vols. Berlin 1845-46.[Addresses to the German Nation, English translation by R. F. Jones and G. H. Turnbull, Chicago 1922].

Fishman, Joshua A. 1972. *Language and Nationalism.* Rowley, Mss.: Newbury House.

Gandhi, Mohandas K. 1965. *Our Language Problem.* Ed. by A. T. Hingorani, Bombay: Bharatiya Vidya Bhavan.

Gottsched, Johan Christoph. [2]1749. Grundlegung einer Deutschen Sprachkunst. *Ausgewählte Werke*, P. M. Mitchel, ed. Berlin, New York: De Gruyter 1979.

Haarmann, Harald. 1975. *Soziologie und Politik der Sprachen Europas.* Munich: Deutscher Taschenbuch Verlag.

Haugen, Einar. 1973. The Curse of Babel. *Daedalus* 102 (3): 47–57.

Haugen, Einar. 1985. The Language of Imperialism: Unity or Pluralism? in: N. Wolfson and Joan Manes, eds. *Language of Inequality.* Berlin, New York, Amsterdam: Mouton, 3–17.

Hellmann-Rajanayagam, D. 1983. Cultural Nationalism and Cultural Identity: The Tamilians in India, Sri Lanka and Malaysia. *Ethnic Studies Report* 1, 2: 14–19.

Humboldt, Wilhelm von. 1830–1835. Ueber die Verschiedenheit des menschlichen Sprachbaus und ihren Einfluss auf die geistige Entwicklung des Menschengeschlechts. In: *Werke in fünf Bänden, III Schriften zur Sprachphilosophie*, A. Flinter and K. Giel, eds.1963. Stuttgart: Cottasche Buchhandlung.

Humboldt, Wilhelm von. 1823. Ueber den Nationalcharacter der Sprachen. In: *Werke in fünf* Bänden, III Schriften zur *Sprachphilosophie*, A. Flinter and K. Giel, eds. 1963. Stuttgart: Cottasche Buchhandlung.

Jacob, James E. and David C. Gordon. 1985. Language Policy in France. In: W.R. Beer and J.E. Jacob, eds. *Language Policy and National Unity*. Totowa, N.J.: Rowman & Allanheld, 106–133.

Jespersen, Otto. 1946. *Mankind, Nation and Individual from a Linguistic Point of view*. London: Allen and Unwin (2 1954).

Jupp, James. 1978. *Sri Lanka - Third World Democracy*. London: Frank Cass.

Kachru, Braj B. 1983. Models for New Englishes. In: J. Cobarrubias, J. A. Fishman, eds. *Progress in Language Planning*. Berlin, New York, Amsterdam: Mouton, 145–170.

Kedourie, Elie. 1960. *Nationalism*. London: Hutchinson 1961.

Kelman, Herbert C. 1971. Language as an Aid and Barrier to Involvement in the National System. In: J. Rubin, B. Jernudd eds. *Can Language be Planned?* Honolulu: The University Press of Hawaii, 21–51.

Klopstock, Friedrich Gottlieb. 1774. *Die Deutsche Gelehrtenrepublik*. R. M. Hurlebusch, ed. Berlin, New York: De Gruyter 1975.

Kloss, Heinz. 1952. *Die Entwicklung neuer germanischer Kultursprachen von 1800 bis 1950*. München: Pohl & Co.

Le Page, R. B. 1964. *The National Language Question*. London, New York: Oxford University Press.

Leibniz, Gottfried Wilhelm. 1697. Unvorgreifliche Gedanken betreffend die Ausübung und Verbesserung der deutschen Sprache [Preliminary thoughts concerning the use and improvement of the German language]. In: *G. W. Leibniz Deutsche Schriften*, ed. W. Schmied-Kowarzik, Leipzig 1916.

Leibniz, Gottfried Wilhelm. 1683. Ermahnung an die Deutschen [Admonition to the Germans]. In: *G. W. Leibniz Deutsche Schrifte*n, ed. W. Schmied-Kowarzik, Leipzig 1916.

Le Tage, R. B. 1964. *The National Language Question: Linguistic Problems of Newly Independent States*. London: Oxford University Press.

Lowenberg, Peter. 1987. Malay in Indonesia, Malaysia, and Singapore: Three Faces of a National Language. In this volume, 146–179.

Minogue, K. R. 1967. *Nationalism*. New York: Basic Books.

Panikkar, K. M. 1969. *Asia and Western Dominance*. Collier Books.

Pattanayak, D. P. 1985. Diversity in Communication and Languages; Predicament of a Multilingual National State: India, a Case Study. In: N. Wolfson, J. Manes, eds. *Language of Inequality*. Berlin, New York, Amsterdam: Mouton, 399–407.

Platt, J., H. Weber, M.L. Ho. 1984. *The New Englishes*. London: Routledge and Kegan Paul.

Senghor, Léopold Sédar. 1956. L'Esprit de la civilisation ou les lois de la culture négro-africaine. Paris: Présence Africaine.

Smith, Anthony D. 1981. *The Ethnic Revival*. London: Cambridge University Press.

Spencer, John W. 1974. Colonial Language Policies and their Legacies in Sub-Saharan Africa. In: J. A. Fishman, ed. *Advances in Language Planning*. The Hague: Mouton. 163–175.

Srivastava, R. N. 1979. Language Movements against Hindi as an Official Language. In: E. Annamalai, ed. *Language Movements in India*. Mysore: Central Institute of Indian Languages, 80–90.

Strevens, Peter. 1983. The Localized Forms of English. In: Braj B. Kachru, ed. *The Other Tongue. English across Cultures*. Oxford: Pergamon Press, 23–30.

Weinstein, Brian. 1979. Language Strategists: Redefining Political Frontiers on the Basis of Linguistic Choices. *World Politics* 31/3, 345–364.

To the Language Born: Thoughts on the Problem of National and International Languages

Jacob Mey

Introduction

There are various ways of approaching the 'national language problem'. The *first* is to deny that there is such a thing as a problem: we all know what national languages are; they are embodied in our institutions, codified in our national legislation, and represented in our consciousness of ourselves as a nation. This I will call the *nationalist*-extremist position.

Another approach takes the opposite tack. Since the concept of nation itself is such a befuddled one, there is not the slightest sense in talking about a/the national language. There are no national languages; *the* national language is a fiction. This I will call the *anti-nationalist* extreme.

Between the nationalist and the anti-nationalist extremes, however, there must be a reasonable middle. The point is how to define that intermediate position: and to do this not just by reference to the extremes from which it is distinguished, but by giving it a positive content of its own.

25

In the following, then, I will assume that there are such things as national languages, but I will not from the outset tie myself down to one particular *definiens*, such as the concept of nation, people, territory, history, etc. All these (as well as some other) conceptual entities play a role in defining our concept, but none of them, taken by itself, is sufficient for providing a workable definition of *national language*.

National Language and Individual Consciousness

In this section, I will concentrate on the basic fact that the concept of a national language is a well-established one among the peoples of what we usually call the 'civilized' world. That is to say, the concept is not well-established by reference to its *intension*, but rather by its *extensional* relations to other concepts. Among the latter, the one that comes most easily to mind is that of *dialect*, here understood in the general sense of: a variety of a (national) language that is spoken (usually not written) in a restricted environment, such as the home or family, the peer group, the local surroundings, or the like. The following may serve to illustrate what I am referring to.

First, an excerpt from an interview with KB, a native speaker of Norwegian, on Jan. 28, 1985. The speaker is an educated woman in her mid 30's, living in a rural community of Telemark county, S. Norway. She was born and raised, and went to school in another urban part of S. Norway, viz. one of the industrial-commercial agglomerations on the East side of the Oslofjord, in Østfold county. At the time of the interview, she had been living in Telemark county for approximately 14 years.

(The following is a transcript (more or less verbatim) of a conversation with the author of this article: the interviewee was given the opportunity of checking the transcript for correctness).

"JM: I noticed you used the word *sparkstøtning* [a popular means of transportation in the winter, consisting basically of a highbacked chair on long gliders]—isn't that rather formal? [Personally, I(JM) never say anything but *sparkstøtting* or *spark*, as most people shorten it]. How's that?

KB: In school, they always told us not to use this or that form. Only now, living here [in Seljord, a rural center in Telemark county], where people speak a dialect, I feel free to speak my own language. But I use many words that are not mine, such as people around here use; when I write a letter, reading it through I find that I use almost every allowed form on the books, and some others as well. My language is a real mixture, but I don't feel cramped any more. Of course, when I go to the city [Oslo], I try to sound more polite, speak nicely, like they taught me at school . . .

JM: So you use formal language along with informal. Is there any rule?

KB: They [the school people] always made us feel inferior, since we weren't allowed to use our dialect, but had to use the 'correct' forms. See, now I say *sjøl* ['self'], and it is only now that I can say this, feeling free to do so. Before, I used to feel I should say *selv* [the 'correct' form, for certain speakers] . . .

JM: But you do feel there's somebody up there who lays down the law—this you *can* say and this you *can't?*

KB: I can't understand who makes these laws. Look, even 'important' people from around where I come from, such as this fellow Apenes [a lawyer and author from Frederikstad, Østfold, and a Conservative MP], he is so well-known, on TV all the time, but when you listen closely, it's all there, no matter how hard he tries, the nasal sounds, the broad *a*'s, the palatalized *l*'s—but why is he trying to speak 'correctly' in the first place? Shouldn't it be alright for him, too, to be from here [i.e. KB's home town, not the place she's living now] . . .?

JM: So what's wrong with your language?

KB: Everybody seems to agree that our dialect is the ugliest of all Norwegian dialects. And everybody agrees that dialects like *Sognemål* or *Vossing* [the dialects of Sogn county, resp. the region around Voss; both in the West of Norway] are *so* beautiful—and yet nobody 'understands' what these people say. Us, they understand but despise: they say that we don't really speak Norwegian but rather some kind of Danish. That's the worst thing about it—that they don't accept us as good Norwegians . . .

JM: So, in a way, you feel that what these people say, sets you apart from the rest of the nation. But what is a nation, anyway?

KB: That's the kind of stuff we used to write essays about in High School! But no matter how you try to define it, it always escapes definition, and you find yourself thrashing around in circles. But we felt that it was very wrong of them to call us Danes because of our language. If anything, we're much closer to Sweden, also language-wise . . .

Funny though, as kids, we used to say that we'd rather die than marry a man speaking a dialect—just imagine, you couldn't understand what your husband said! And then, of course, we didn't realize that *we* spoke a dialect, too . . .

JM: So now you feel more proud of your dialect than you used to?

KB: You know what, some time ago this theater critic [the late Erik Pierstorff in *Dagbladet,* a Liberal, Oslo-based newspaper] reviewed a satirical comedy, opening at the *Norske Teater* (the *nynorsk* scene (on *nynorsk,* see below) in Oslo]. It was written in the dialect of my home [the industrial-commercial agglomeration of Sarpsborg/Frederikstad]. And he remarked that he couldn't see the point of using precisely this dialect—it had neither wit nor charm, he said . . .

JM: What do you think will happen to the dialects in Norway?

KB: Well, I'll tell you something. Quite close to here there's a place called Edland—200 people living quite isolated and speaking a real old-fashioned dialect until recently. But now, with TV covering more and more of Norway, these people are starting to speak like the rest of us. That's a pity, I think.

Also, at Bø [the local shopping and school center for the lower parts of Telemark county] they're considering establishing *bokmøl* classes now, where up till now they only have had *nynorsk* in the schools. Naturally, the *nynorsk* people are very worried, but what can they do?" [*bokmøl* and *nynorsk* are the two official ('national') languages of Norway; the former is predominant in the urban areas and most of the press; the latter is supported by the majority of Norwegians living in rural parts of the county (around 20% of the population in 1975)].

The second excerpt is from a recent Norwegian novel (Brantenberg 1985: 64–65). The two interlocutors are Beate, a

15-year old girl from a working-class environment, who goes to the City High School, and her mother. In her freshman year, Beate becomes conscious of the 'ugly' language she and her surroundings use, and contrasts this with what the teachers at her school try to inculcate into their students as the 'correct' standard. (Notice in particular the author's fine irony in letting Beate make use of the very forms she has been taught to ostracize, in order to condemn all 'wrong' language (cf. *ille, orda* in the text below).

"It's ugly to say *ho* ['she'; for *hun*], Beate said, —and it's wrong to say *ille* ('very'; literally: 'badly'), and it's terribly (*ille* [!]) vulgar to say *bøtær* and *bilær* and *bussær* ('boats', 'cars', 'buses'; for *båter, biler, busser*), and all sorts of things that we have been saying all the time; that's not how we should have talked, and *-a* at the end of all the words (*orda* [!]), we have to stop saying that, and Frederikstad people, they use the wrong language as soon as they open their mouths, especially here on Chapel Rock (*Kapellfjellet;* [a low-class housing environment away from the city center]). Now I will train myself to talk nice."

"Is that what you're learning over at school?"

"Yes. There are lots of funny dialects in Norway, and people all over say the strangest things. But the way we talk in this town, that's not a dialect. That's just plain wrong. Do you understand?"

"No. Is that what your teacher's telling you?"

"Yes. For example . . ." etc.

What we can learn from the above excerpts is the following:

(a) Even though Norwegian dialects (or at least some of them) are considered 'beautiful', etc., the amount of prestige involved in using a dialect, as compared to using the standard language, is very limited.

(b) The standard language(s), as taught in the schools, is (are) felt by learners to be a roadblock on the way to full linguistic self-realization. In the case of KB, this latter achievement came only *after* she moved out of her original linguistic area, and years after she finished her education. But also in her case, the influence and prestige of the norms taught in the schools continue to prevail, even against her own newly-won freedom and consciousness.

(c)   In the case of Norway, the situation is, of course, a bit more complicated than in countries recognizing only one standard. Norway, as is well known, has *two* official languages, *bokmål* and *nynorsk* (cf. above). Within these two main languages, local varieties of different prestige obtain; quite obviously, the (rural) varieties of *nynorsk* are usually perceived as quaint, rather than ugly, and even if they do not confer a lot of social prestige, they are not socially discriminated against. Quite the opposite is the case for those (urban) dialects that are said to 'pertain to' *bokmål* (for whatever such an ascription is worth). These are, in many cases, considered not only as ugly, but vulgar and stupid; they are socially downgrading. Cases in point are the local dialects of the Eastern wards of the city of Oslo, the dialects of the industrial towns on both sides of the Oslofjord (also here a clear negative bias towards the East), the rural districts of certain parts of Southeastern Norway (especially Østfold and Hedmark counties), and so on. Conversely, there are almost no dialects that, *as such*, lend prestige to their speakers (a few notable exemptions are certain urban dialects of the South, and of course the dialect of the city of Bergen in the West, albeit here, too, with numerous exceptions and restrictions). The only 'dialect' (if we may call it that) which carries instant remuneration in the form of social esteem and greater acceptability, is the language which invariably is ornated with the *epitheton* 'cultivated', or, in a more sweeping way of speaking, 'nice', as opposed to 'ugly': two adjectives that crop up time and again in any discussion on dialects and 'correct' use of language, and of course not exclusively among speakers of Norwegian. (This is especially clear in the second excerpt above; cf. Gulliksen (1979)).

(d)   The crucial paradox in all this seems to be that whereas the schools make every effort to teach their students a 'nice' language, it is still the case that for the majority of the latter language never becomes anything but a straitjacket, to be donned or doffed, given the proper occasion. Even among the 'successful' minority, there will be many who spend years and years in liberating themselves linguistically, and then only at the price of mixing together "all allowed forms," as my interviewee KB puts it; that is, the tyranny of the standard dialect can only be done away with at the price of abandoning all norms whatsoever. (On the attractions of "talking ugly," see the interesting inquiry by Gulliksen (1979)).

Dialect or language: The national standard

If the evidence in the previous section is considered from the two extreme positions sketched above in the *Introduction* to this article, we see that neither is able to make a convincing case, even though both contain an element of truth.

The *nationalist* will point out that the existence of a standard 'dialect', even though it is only imperfectly realized in most cases, documents the legitimacy and necessity of a national language as the norm for all dialects.

The *anti-nationalist* will argue that precisely this fact, viz. that the national norm only exists as an abstract system of rules, realized, at best, in a dwindling minority of native speakers, illustrates the uselessness of the whole concept of a 'national language'.

As I said before, both positions cannot be true at the same time, since they contradict each other. This 'external' contradiction, as one may call it, is borne out by an 'internal' weakness common to both concepts: their linkage to the idea of a 'nation'. It is certainly true that the original concept of 'nation' had something to do with the idea of being 'born into' certain properties, rights, and duties, among these the ability to speak a language 'natively'. However, the 'nation' concept, when used about language, fails to carry over to the modern nation-state, the latter being the product of a much more recent development. The national state, as such, never really was established until the beginning of the Modern Age for most European countries (Italy and Germany being among the more notorious come-lately's in this respect).

As an illustration, consider the fact that the original Latin *(Vulgata)* version of the Bible uses both *populi* and *gentes* (the latter usually narrowed down to mean 'gentiles', as the equivalent of the Hebrew *goyim,* and in fact often translated, for lack of a better equivalent, as 'nations'), whereas Latin *natio* usually has a tribal as well as a linguistic connotation. The author of the *Acts of the Apostles,* in the famous scene (2:4–13) where different people are said to be hearing the miracles of God, "every man [sic!] in our own tongue, wherein we were born," by a kind of divinely-organized (and in itself miraculous) simultaneous translation, uses precisely the word *natio (viri religiosi ex omni natione quae sub caelo est);* and the sacred text immediately links this up with the notion of 'being born' *(natus)* in(to) a language *(audivimus unusquisque linguam nostram, in qua nati sumus).* Similarly in Classical Latin, *natio* is used (as, e.g., by Caesar in *De Bello Gallico*) in the sense of 'tribe': 'a band of people linked together by common "language, institutions, and laws'" *(lingua, institutis, legibus;* B.G. I: 1). Whereas the Roman *nation* always is referred to by Caesar as *populus Romanus,* the Gauls are a *natio,* distinguished, among other things, by their dedication to all things religious *(cp.: natio . . . Gallorumm admodum dedita religionibus;* B.G. VI: 16).

During the Middle Ages (and for a long time after), the universities organized their students by 'nations', i.e. what we today perhaps would call 'ethnic groupings'; a relic of this is still found in today's Swedish and Finnish universities, where the student body *(studentkåren)* divides up its members according to their native counties or regions: any such subdivision is still called a *nation* in Swedish (in the Finnish equivalent *osakunta,* liter. 'part-body', the historic allusion has been lost).

The trouble with the concept of 'national language' is that it refers to an historical state of affairs which is no longer existent. As so often is the case, history outruns language, or alternatively, people omit to adjust their language to the changed environments, persisting in using the old terms for new things, putting "new wine into old bottles," with the well-known disastrous results (St. Luke 5:37).

Whereas the old idea of 'nation' directly related to "language, [religious] institutions, and laws" (as witnessed by the classical authors), with the advent of the 'national state' we are confronted with a quite different concept: that of the people organized (or organizing themselves) into administrative units with fixed boundaries, a central authority, and cultural, rather than strictly linguistic homogeneity. Thus, the former New England colonies, on achieving independence, referred to themselves as "one nation indivisible under God" *(Preamble to the Constitution)*, but adopted, as their official name, the much more appropriate *United States*. And so we have the paradox that words like *nation, national,* currently are used to refer to all sorts of institutions and concepts that, properly speaking, are as far removed from the old 'nation' as is the modern 'state' itself (think of expressions such as *across the nation, nationwide, national security,* or even the (strictly denumerable) set n^{th} *national Bank of X,* where n is a natural number (usually ≤ 5), and X may represent any element within the (local) geographical universe).

Against this backdrop, it makes no sense to speak of a 'national language', unless we mean something entirely different from the old concept: 'a language spoken by a certain group of people called a nation'. No wonder then, too, that we have 'nations' (in the modern sense of 'nation-state') with more than one language, something which would be excluded under the primitive one-to-one relationship of 'nation' and 'institution' (in the widest sense of the term). The case of Norway that I referred to above, section 1, serves to illustrate this: here, one has two national languages with equal rights, guaranteed in all official and legal contexts. And, of course, the case is by no means unique: in Switzerland, we have as many as *four* national languages (of which the fourth, Romansh, only recently has come into full recognition, as witnessed by the fact that from 1976 on, Swiss money bills carry a fourfold legend of languages where there used to be the three major ones only: French, Italian, and German). Or, to take an extreme case: would anybody dare to name the 'national language' of a country like Nigeria? The most we can say here is that we have an official language, adopted by the *state* for its business across the *nation*—but what is this 'nation'? And whose is 'the' national language, anyway?[1]

A 'National Language': ideology or reality?

Having established the impossibility of dealing with the concept of 'national language' on a simple, realistic level, like: What does it (universally or locally) refer to? or: Where does it come from?, we may now try to determine it in other, perhaps more subtle ways. Or, to put it differently: we cannot just kill the 'nation' as the *definiens* for 'national language' and leave it at that. The very variety of the ways this concept is used, points at its importance and viability—even though it may not commend itself by virtues like well-definedness. Or, maybe more precisely: Whenever we seem to have to do with a well-defined case of a 'national language', e.g. in the form of descriptions, teaching materials, or other literature (e.g. anthologies), making explicit or implicit reference to the concept of a 'national', or even 'supranational' language, as the case may be, the fortunate object of that honorific appellation turns out to be a particular dialect, commended by high prestige or otherwise.

A typical instance is Chao's (1925) description of the "Chinese National Language," a pioneering work in that it used gramophone recordings at a time when the Linguaphone method hadn't even begun to overcome its childhood's diseases; yet also a living testimony to the hegemony claims that usually are inherent in terms such as 'national': the 'national language,' as described by Chao, is nothing but the dialect of Peking! (see Gal'cev 1962: 116).[2]

The question before us now is to decide how to characterize the 'national language', if it cannot be ascribed to the nation, that mythical beast. Should we simply declare it to be a by-product of ideology, to be discarded as a useless chimaera?

The answer to this first question is both easy to give, and hard to account for. Of course, the 'national language' is not to be done away with by administrative, educational, or scientific *fiat*. But on the other hand, it cannot be understood without reference to ideology. If we just were to call it a useful piece of ideological home industry, not to be taken too seriously, another question, of course, still remains, namely, for whom that particular piece of ideology may be useful. Naturally, these two questions cannot be separated.

Human language is the realization of human consciousness. We take cognizance of our world by establishing conceptual relationships, and realizing these in the shape of words, sentences, and texts. Conversely, our 'wording', as I call it (for this concept and its definition, see Mey 1985, esp. ch. 3.2), influences our praxis: conscious praxis becomes praxis of consciousness, and the practice thusly consecrated ("conscienticized," to use a term coined by Freire (1968)) in its turn influences our wording. This continuous, dialectic movement is the basic presupposition for all language, both in its origin and its use. However, the dialectics is not by any means a merely 'spiritual' one. Praxis is what is the *matter*, in the strict sense of the word: What matters is the material world to which our words extend, and from which they come back, laden with the enrichment of material praxis. However, this praxis is also a fight to continue an existence against all odds, a controversy where, no matter how well we practice our wording and word our practice, Nature *will* have the last word: "That is the end of the world news," in Anthony Burgess' phrase (1982:x).

If we consider a nation as a group of people working together to realize their 'practical' aims (this is not a definition, but at best a rather ingenuous assumption), then we could metaphorically consider the nation's 'Gross Cultural Product' as represented in language by some means of 'culture production.' Of course, there are other 'products', too, but none of them are as all-pervasive of our culture, and as encompassing, as language (at least not in our present, Western civilization). However, just as in the case of the nation's *economic* production, there are important differences, too, in the roles which society allots to its individual members in the process of *cultural* production. People come into this world in all kinds, with widely differing capacities and possibilities, for material as for cultural production; and so the question is not only to be born, but to be born into the right class. As the old saying goes: Once a 'have-not', always a 'have-not' (exceptions notwithstanding). And if you're one of the 'haves', born into wealth and glory, you're certainly not interested in sharing all that with the 'have-nots'. The praxis of the affluent is meant to guarantee their riches, to increase rather than disperse them. The cultural product that reflects this practice is similarly geared towards conserving the *status quo* that favors the rich, not towards promoting revolution-ary thinking. Thus we find that in every period of history, the well-to-do protect themselves, not only by physically oppressing the poor, but by planting cultural hedges around their 'property', erecting educational and other roadblocks on the paths giving access to the higher layers of society.

Knowledge, as we all know, represents power. Knowing how to perform a certain operation not only enables me to play a role in the production of the goods that are necessary for my survival—it makes it also possible for me to keep the others out, by withhold-ing that knowledge from them, or at least controlling their access to it. This is true both of the knowledge that goes into purely physical products, and of that knowledge which is a prerequisite for orga-nizing the material production on a higher level (technical and industrial 'know-how'). It is also true of those processes which, directly or indirectly, in reality or ideology, influence and steer the overall planning of society's material and cultural existence. To describe those processes, we use words like religion, culture, science, philosophy, literature, art, and so on. The most interest-ing question to ask about them is not "where do they all come from" (like one is wont in those eternal, and indeed somewhat jaded quarrels on 'base' and 'superstructure' in certain trends of the Marxist dialogue). The important aspect that unites all these 'products' is their being manifestations of human consciousness, their constituting embodiments of conscienticized human praxis that in some, or maybe all, ways depend upon, and are repre-sented by language. In this sense, language is the true constituent of all higher forms of society: It represents society for itself and by itself. In the strictest sense of the word, language *legitimates* society: Language lays down the law inasmuch as it represents the steering principles of human consciousness in human praxis.

This intimate association between the 'language of the realm' and the latter's governing consciousness (its ideology, if one wants to call it that) branches out in two directions: Diachronically, the traditional possession of the 'cultural values' (used here as a cover term) by the ruling classes is not an accident of history, but an ontogenetic necessity; synchronically, the control exercised by the ruling classes of society in cultural matters imposes itself as a visible check on language, its system and use.

The fact that language control came into vogue precisely at the onset of the capitalistic era is by no means accidental (unless one wants to call it an 'accident of history', which, properly speaking, is a contradiction in itself). The diverse 'Academies' that have burgeoned across Europe in newer history were (unlike their predecessor-in-name, the Athenian Academy of Plato and his friends) no mere debating clubs or philosophical walking guilds: They were from the beginning (and consciously) endowed with the power of censuring, hence of ruling and legislation. That is, they were the means by which the emerging rulers endeavored (in most cases, successfully) to confirm their rising consciousness as the future *arbiters*, not just of the arts, but of society itself.[3] Yet, the rules they laid down were no 'arbitrary' instruments of power display; they had a very distinct function, viz., to channel and direct the new consciousness of society, of which language was the prime expression. In this way, a double purpose was served: One, the 'cultural heritage' (read: the ideology legitimating the division of societal power) was safeguarded; two, any effort at a revolutionary overthrow of the existing power structures could be nipped in the bud.

The single standard

The most efficient way to control any process at all is to constantly supervise it. However, this is usually impossible: there are other things in life than supervision, and the show must go on. So instead, you introduce the *check:* Either as a point in time/space through which the process must pass (as in the case of a military or customs checkpoint), or by setting up a body of rules according to which the process must be performed, whereupon you inculcate these rules by force or instill them by persuasion. The latter method has the additional advantage (if it is successful, that is) of gradually eliminating the need for direct control altogether: Instead of actively supervising a particular process yourself, you can delegate your power to the rules that are built into the persons performing the process.

There is one condition, though. Or rather, there are two, but they are usually collapsed into one: The rules must be unique and they must be yours. If the rules leave room for voluntary decisions on the part of the performers, you can never be sure which way the process eventually will be going. Especially in big operations, like joint military or economic enterprises, this is an absolutely crucial condition. On the other hand, you must be sure that the rules faithfully reflect your view of the process, as far as its implementation and ultimate aims are concerned. If somebody from the outside manages to pervert the rule system, you can be sure of one thing: That will *not* be to your advantage, but to his or hers.

The steering of the cultural processes, inasmuch as these embody the governing consciousness of our society, is a matter of no small importance. The rulers of society, that is, the people who profit from the way society is organized and who would stand to lose enormously if things were to change, have every interest in keeping the current governing consciousness alive and well. Language, as the most powerful instrument of forming and expressing that consciousness (the "wording of the world," alluded to earlier), enjoys the same importance. Linguistic rules are no trivial matter in our society: Grammar is a real "tyrant," as I have called it elsewhere (Mey 1979). The reason for its power lies in the importance of the linguistic 'checks', both as continuity-preserving measures and as defenders of a monopoly. If I can disqualify a potential opponent by reference to his or her 'bad accent' or faulty orthography, I will already have won a minor victory. But if I can keep that person out of the circles of influence altogether, e.g. by putting up signs of "No Admission" ("except for duly accredited persons"), I will be able to sit on my privileges for ever.

The functioning of these cultural 'hedges' depends to a large degree on whether we can define a standard for our culture that poses as universal, but in reality is the proper privilege, native or by education, of the selected few. And since in our society, access to educational privileges has become increasingly more important than birth-rights, taken by themselves, the importance of the language rules has increased, too. Access to education is, of course, in many cases a matter of being able to pay your school fees. But on top of it, the educational system favors those with the correct social and economic background. Not because that background in itself carries weight (in a democracy, all backgrounds should theoretically be equal; however, remember Orwell!), but since such a background carries with it a certain set of the mind, reflected in an acceptance of the way our society has organized itself, in particular the standards that it imposes. Respect for rules, in particular for the rules of grammar, is a 'birth-mark' of the upper and middle classes in our society, and an extremely important ingredient of the 'hidden' curriculum of our institutions of education (and the higher the education, the more important this curriculum tends to be, at the same time that it becomes gradually more hidden). Language standards are an integrated part of this system; as such, they have a definite controlling task in our society.

National or Standard?

From what I have said so far, it has become clear that the main motivation for, as well as the main value of the 'national language' concept is its character of a *standard* for all users. I have argued that such a standard, although in principle established for all of the people (in our times even, as in the case of Chinese after the 1911 revolution, by means of so-called democratic procedures, such as the voting-by-majority in a conference of representative delegates), still expresses the norms and beliefs of the very few, viz., those for whom a certain, now defunct political philosophy had devised the name of 'culture-bearers': The cultural and economic elite.

Thus, the 'Nation' becomes implicitly identical with the 'ruling class', just as the 'educated language', which is taken as the basis for the legalized system of rules, belongs to those who have had the privilege of an education, thereby eliminating all those who, for reasons of economy, geographical distance, or working and housing conditions, have been unable to 'get themselves' that education. (And if they do obtain an education, it is of course, still on the premises laid down for them by those others)[4]

My thesis is, therefore, that we should 'unmask', debunk the concept of 'national' language, and instead talk about a 'standard', imposed on the users of the 'national' languages by the State's powerful, its institutions and classes. The advantage of such an approach is that it pulls away the ideological veil surrounding the concept of 'nation'. You can argue about a standard, but the idea of a 'nation' is unarguable, for a variety of reasons (some of which I have mentioned above). Thus, the hidden oppression, implicit in the notion 'national' (cf. the quote in the interview above on "not being a good Norwegian"), can be brought into the open and finally done away with.

The question whether or not we *need* a standard for language (use) has not been explicitly discussed so far. Neither will I do this in the sequel, but only point out one interesting aspect that could change the tenor of the old arguments *pro et con*.

In discussing the relative advantages of different grammatical models, we used to put a great deal of emphasis on 'naturalness' and 'simplicity'. These qualities were thought of, first of all, as theoretical assets of certain models. The more 'natural' or 'simple' a model, the better the theory behind it was thought to be. But in the sequel, these notions carried over to other fields of interest as well: for instance, a 'natural' and 'simple' grammatical model was thought of as indispensable in conceptualizing what was going on in the process of language acquisition (either by first, or second, third, etc. language learners). From simple model to 'simplified' grammar, however, the road is a very short one; hence, the advocates of such pedagogical monstrosities as 'Basic English' joined hands with those who defended the 'simple standard', e.g. in speaking and spelling (cf. the various 'simplified' spelling movements which created, as their main effect, more, rather than less, confusion in matters of orthography and 'language feel'). In general, however, the idea of standardizing human speech in the interest of better communication is about just as profound as the notion that we should communicate with a computer in digital or octal (or even, God forbid, make our brains function that way!)

Moreover, the standard that is purportedly indispensable for our understanding a message is, first of all, the *written* language's (cf. all the arguments stressing the value of a standardized orthography). The claim that "people wouldn't understand each other if there weren't some kind of a standard" holds strictly only for written communication; in oral interaction, it seldom happens that people with enough social clout to demand to be understood, don't get the message across, standard or no standard.

But suppose now most of our written communication takes

place by computer—which surely is not an improbable perspective for the next few decades. Wouldn't we then be able to let the computer standardize our output, rather than continue to have the familiar bore and scourge of spelling and other standards as a requirement on successful communication between individuals? De-ideologized, i.e. class- and otherwise sanitized routines could take the brunt off educational privileges and their effects, stressing the latter's purely *instrumental* character of providing access routes to individual and social communication. Nobody could be discriminated against because of a faulty orthography, simply because the need to spell correctly would henceforth be redefined as a mechanical requirement, embodied in computerized spelling routines, much like the already existing ones, but without all their imperfections and shortcomings. We may deplore the downfall of spelling as a handicraft, in the same way that we, from a purely esthetical point of view, may lament the decay of the art of calligraphy ever since the advent of the typewriter and its successor, the computerized printing device. However, one thing is certain: Today, no one who is applying for a job will receive preferential treatment because of a nice handwriting; it is a quaint employer who will choose a person on the grounds of a beautifully handwritten application alone—*ceteris paribus*, of course, and disregarding the possible graphological aspects of job-screening. A privilege has gone down the drain along with a craft; nothing for nothing in this world.

National or international? Conclusion

In this final section, I want to consider a practical aspect of linguistic standardization, or more correctly, of enforcing a 'national' linguistic standard (whatever that means or implies) on people of other linguistic backgrounds.[5] Standardization, in this connection, often comes close to discrimination; and its main instrument are the language tests that often block for an alien's acquiring a permanent residence permit or citizenship in his/her new country of residence. While it makes some sense to ensure that people can understand and use the language of the country where they want to spend their lives, the way these tests often are administered makes them look more like convenient, one-way barriers than sensible road-stations on the way to integration into the new community (for details, see Skutnabb-Kangas 1981).

But the problem of non-natives speaking a language that, although not their own, yet in many ways is as important for them (or even more important) as (than) their native tongue, is by no means limited to discriminatory measures against immigrant workers. There are mainly two kinds of surroundings in which this problem-tangle gets activated: The first is the area of foreign language instruction; the second is that of what I will call 'International English'.

As to the first, I will restrict myself to a reference. Research in the theory of foreign language acquisition has lately begun to be interésted in the non-standard varieties that non-native speakers construct during acquisition of a 'second mother tongue'. Such 'interlanguages', as they are called, have been unequivocally determined (e.g. by Wagner 1983) as being valuable intermediate, yet important steps in acquiring a language and in 'wording' the world (cf. above). Any strict application of standard criteria for correctness in such a context makes, of course no sense at all.

But the buck doesn't stop here. Most, not to say all, second language acquirers will never make the 'standard' in all respects—but on reflection, how many natives do, and why should *they* be treated more leniently and understandingly as regards this kind of requirement? Besides, even native users may, given the proper occasion, feel themselves less strictly obliged to a rigorous observance of the "grammatical tyrant's" rules. Nash (1982) recounts the experiences of a 'displaced' native speaker of American English who, having lived for several years in a foreign environment (Puerto Rico), observes that "strict adherence to conventional English spelling practices at all times" seems less and less essential: on the contrary, such fidelity is experienced as "both unnecessary and troublesome" (Nash 1982: 259). Clearly, what is sauce to the native goose is also good for the ungrammatical gander (or vice versa, as the case may be).

There are, however, important groups of second (third, . . ., etc.) language users that neither are immigrants, nor aspire to living their lives in foreign surroundings: I mean the numerous people that, for some reason or other, have to use non-native languages in order to communicate with native speakers of those languages, either in their daily business, or at least on special, usually important occasions.

As an instance of the former case, consider all those whose native tongues or dialects are permanently and irrevocably defined as being outside the 'civilized', standardized language community. One can think of tribal languages in most countries of Africa, much of the Americas, or even Europe; for instance, the third language of Norway, Samic (or Lapp, as it used to be called by non-natives) is still not recognized as one of the official languages of the country; the fourth language of Switzerland has had a lot of problems, too (cf. what I have said earlier). But all this is peanuts compared, e.g., to what native North-African speakers of Berber must go through in their communication with government organs above the strictly local level: Without a minimal knowledge of Arabic or French, or without the assistance of a knowledgeable intermediary, such persons will never get anywhere in dealing with 'their' authorities.

The other group I'm thinking of in this connection are the people that, for reasons such as business or scientific contacts, political conferences and meetings (yes, and even touristic purposes!) have to use a medium of communication that is not their own. Lately, a number of people (among these the Japanese linguist Takao Suzuki, and also the author of these lines) have become interested in the problems that face users of (mainly) English in their contacts with native, as well as with fellow non-native speakers of that particular language. Typically, what happens is this: The non-native, user of 'International English' (the term is Suzuki's; pers. comm.) feels discriminated against when native speakers, because of their greater fluency and ease, completely drown out what he/she has to say. On top of that, the stark 'non-nativeness' of such a person's accent is perceived, both by the speaking subjects themselves and by their interlocutors, as detracting from the content of what he/she is trying to convey.

There are, of course, people who will argue that "If you speak a language other than your own, you have to emulate, or at least try and imitate, a native standard." But this brings up not only the problem of how to choose among the various, existing native standards of a language (such as American vs. British usage in the case of English), but furthermore, the requirement is as illusory as it is unfair. Barring non-understandability, the non-native should not be forced to conform to (a) standard(s) that not even the majority of (let alone all) native speakers adhere to (cp. the pretensions of some local teachers of English in a country like Denmark, who seriously believe that they are bringing up their students in 'Oxford English'!) Rather than forcing the non-native speakers' hands, we should recognize the existence of 'non-standard' varieties of languages (all the while taking care not to confuse these with 'sub-standard' ones and distancing ourselves from whatever discriminating purposes the latter term may be put to use for). There will, of course, always be differences in societal importance between such 'non-standard' norms: They can vary all the way from (almost) internationally recognized varieties of English, such as the West African or Indian brands (not to speak of other, still more 'native' reaches of the Old Empire!) to an emerging, not yet quite *arrivé*, member of the 'International English' Club like 'Nipponized English' (see, e.g., Mey 1986 for examples of this so-called 'NE').

The lack of balance in international environments between native and non-native users of an 'international' language could, furthermore, be redressed by stipulating (as Suzuki has suggested (in pers. comm.)) that there simply be introduced a *ban* on the use of native languages by natives in such surroundings. Thus, e.g., English speakers would have to resort to French or Russian, the French would be obliged to express themselves in Chinese or Arabic, and so on. This solution would indeed, at least partially, solve the non-native speakers' problems, even though it would not take care of all their difficulties. Given that, for a long time to come, we probably still will have to have simultaneous translation facilities at major international political or economic conferences, such a policy would still be in keeping with our main objective: To put an end to all discrimination due to the 'linguistic imperialism' of the tongues of the mighty.

Notes

1. Compare also the following instances from languages outside our Western circles:

The Japanese National Language Research Institute in Tokyo is called: *Kokuritsu Kokugo Kenkyūsho*, i.e. literally: 'State Institute of the National Language', where the word *koku* means, primarily, 'state, kingdom', but apparently also functions as the equivalent of 'nation(al)'. Here, 'state' and 'nation' are not even distinguished in their lexical representations. Similarly, in Gal'cev's *Introduction to the Study of Chinese* (1962), one finds the word 'nation(al)' in three different, mutually more or less exclusive surroundings:

(a)   "the Chinese national language" (and, e.g., its dialects; cf. 1962:5)
(b)   "a multination state" (said of the People's Republic of China; *ibid.*)
(c)   "the literary form of the national language" (as opposed to the other form, "based on the norm for spoken language"; *ibid.*: 12). This language is also called the "generally accepted language" *(pu-tun-hua)*.
(d)   "The all-national language *pu-tun-hua*" (ibid.: 19).

From these quotes, it would appear that in a Chinese context, the term 'national' has at least the same double meaning as in Japan: 'belonging to the state', as in 'all-national' (and, by the same token 'generally accepted'); both are translations of Chin. *pu-tōng-hua*: [Gal'cev (1962: 12, 19)]; but that furthermore, the 'national language' is based, first of all, upon the written, literary standard. Clearly, none of these meanings of 'national' make sense together with 'multinational', as in (b); furthermore, the main content of the notion 'national', as in (d) or (a), seems to be its superordinate status, further specified (as in (c)) by reference to the literary standard.

2. The task of the all-nation (!) conference on the future teaching of Chinese that was called in 1912, one year after the Revolution, was to discuss the necessity of introducing the teaching of "the national [literally: 'all-state'] language" (Gal'cev 1962:92); as it proved to be the case, the pronunciation norms that were decided upon (by majority voting!) were obtained by a "mechanical identification of the sounds of the Peking dialect with the sound phenomena of the other dialects" (ibid.: 93–94). This effort at unification, however, never caught on: as Gal'cev remarks (1962:15), the people continued to use their own local dialects. In the end, the official confirmation of this supremacy of the Peking dialect came in 1930-1932, when the 'all-nation' syllabary that had been elaborated by the 1912 conference, was brought to conform with Peking speech. (*ibid.*)

3. Characteristic is the following blunt remark by Boileau, one of the chief 'movers' in the French cultural struggle following the establishment of the *Académie Française* (Boileau was born in its founding year, 1632; his repartee was

sparked by Louis XVI's enthusiasm for a minor work by a forgotten poetaster of the period): "Your Majesty should leave the judgment on these matters to those who are qualified to judge." Rather than having him imprisoned for *lèse-majesté*, the *Roi-Soleil* is said to have followed the advice of his underling, whose words indeed embodied 'the law' (Boileau used to be called *'le législateur du Parnasse'*).

4. Traditionally, in our modern societies, it is especially the written language that most of the time is seen as serving the perpetuation of our culture. Yet, also this truth suffers some qualification.

The Swedish novelist and essayist Frans G. Bengtsson (1981) reflects in his piece 'The long-haired Merovingians' on the supposedly authentic case of the cub football reporter of *The Chicago Herald*, who suddenly finds himself in the awkward position of having to review a performance of Shakespeare's *Othello* for his newspaper. Not knowing anything about literature (he isn't even familiar with the name of Shakespeare!), he describes what he sees on the scene as a football match (though he mentions, in passing, that the piece also could have a message with respect to the problems of racially mixed marriages).

The review was a resounding success—and many people went to see *Othello* who otherwise never would have, and the football reporter was promoted to the literary criticism department of the paper. As Bengtsson remarks, this anecdote shows us the importance of looking at cultural events through noncultural glasses. In my terminology, I would say that the young, inexperienced reporter, without even realizing it, rebelled against the *standardized* interpretation of our culture, as it is embodied in (among other things) our university curricula, and against those persons who, representing the official, institutionalized culture, aspire to a unique knowledge of, and dictatorial authority in, matters of culture (including the use of language).

5. Although this aspect has acquired increased popularity among those that object to the presence of non-native residents among an autochthonous population, I will pass by in silence arguments based on a nationality ideology smacking of nationalism or its dangerously close relative, racism. That *the* national language should be a precondition for 'national' feelings makes no sense in any context. Even for believers in things national, the existence of 'multinational' states (in itself a conceptual enormity) must turn all such considerations into pumpkin meat. Nobody will seriously question the quality of Swiss nationalism, or of patriotic feelings among Norwegians; yet, the Swiss have four national languages, the Norwegians two. Such arguments are only useful when one wants to attack groups of people that are considered undesirable for other (e.g. economic) reasons. This nationalism is just so much ideology, witness the interview quoted at the beginning of this article.

References

Bengtsson, Frans G. 1981. De långhåriga merovingerna. Stockholm: Norstedts. [1955].

Brantenberg, Gerd. 1985. Ved fergestedet. (At the ferry-crossing). Oslo: Aschenhoug.

Burgess, Anthony. 1982. The end of the world news: An entertainment. London: Hutchinson.

Caesar, C. Julius. 1944. De Bello Gallico Libri VII. J. Janssen, ed. Leiden: Brill. [A.D. 63]

Chao, Yuen-Ren. 1925. A phonograph course in the Chinese National Language. Shanghai: Academia Sinica.

Gal'cev, I.N. 1962. Vvedenije v izučenije kitajskogo jazyka. Moskva: Izdatel'stvo literatury na inostrannych jazykach. [Biblioteka filologa]

Freire, Paolo. 1973. Pedagogy of the oppressed. New York: Seabury Press. [1968].

Gulliksen, Torun. 1979. "Det er deiligst å snakke såkalt stygt" [Talking vulgar makes one feel good]. Norsklæeren 2,3:43–46.

Kachru, Braj B. (ed.) 1982. The other tongue: English across cultures. Urbana, IL: University of Illinois Press.

Mey, Jacob. 1979. 'Zur kritischen Sprachtheorie'. In: Jacob Mey (ed.), Pragmalinguistics: Theory and practice. The Hague/Paris/New York: Mouton Publishers. (= Rasmus Rask Studies in Pragmatic Linguistics, Vol. 1 & Janua Linguarum, Series Maior, Vol. 85). pp. 411–432.

Mey, Jacob. 1985. Whose Language? A study in linguistic pragmatics. Amsterdam/Philadelphia: John Benjamins. (= Pragmatics and Beyond Companion Series, Vol. 3).

Mey, Jacob. 1986. Communicational aspects of foreign language instruction. Tsukuba, Ibaraki-ken: Tsukuba University Foreign Language Center Bulletin.

Nash, Rose. 1982. 'Pringlish: Still more language contact in Puerto Rico'. In: Kachru, ed. 1982: 250–269.

Novum Iesu Christi Testamentum iuxta Vulgatam edition is textum. 1939. Rom etc.: Desdée De Brouwer. [A.D. 50–110].

Skutnabb-Kangas, Tove. 1981. Tvåspråkighet [Bilingualism]. Lund: Liber. (Engl. transl.: Bilingualism or not: The education of minorities. Clevedon, Avon, UK: Multilingual Matters, Ltd. 1983).

Wagner, Johs. 1983. Kommunikation und Spracherwerb. Tübingen: Narr.

Swahili as a National Language in East Africa

Marilyn Merritt
and
Mohamed H. Abdulaziz

In this paper we will describe some of the historical background and the current state of affairs regarding the status of Swahili, or perhaps more properly Kiswahili (using the prefixed form that is used when speaking the Swahili language), in East Africa. The geographical spread of Swahili as a *lingua franca* extends beyond East Africa and within Africa is second only to Arabic in terms of its range. However, as this is a book about **national languages** our main focus will be on Kenya and Tanzania, where Swahili is politically designated as the national language with a contrasting discussion of Uganda, where Swahili has assumed a somewhat less prominent role.

In describing the situation here, and noting contrasts within the region, we hope to provide some sense of the major factors that have contributed to the selection of national languages in this region which may be of general interest. We also hope to sharpen the concept of national language by illustrating both the linguistic and socio-political features that must obtain for a language variety in order for it to be *viable* as a national language, especially in a heavily multilingual and multi-cultural setting such as East Africa.

48

Further, we hope to give some sense of the ongoing "competition" between languages in different domains and the concomitant complexity of language choice for individual speakers, although we can only hint at this within the scope of this paper (see, e.g. Abdulaziz 1972, Parkin 1974). Finally, throughout our discussion we hope to convey some sense of the changes that have occurred with Swahili—not only in the patterns of its use, but also in its internal development as a dynamic language.

Historical Overview of East African Nationhood

The modern nation states of Kenya, Tanzania and Uganda all emerged in the 1960's, having gained independence from the colonial government of the United Kingdom. The land area of Kenya covers 224,960 square miles while Tanzania covers 363,708 square miles and Uganda 91,076 square miles. According to the U.N. World Population Chart of 1984 inhabitants number 19,761,000 in Kenya; 21,710,000 in Tanzania, and 15,150,000 in Uganda. All three countries access Lake Victoria, but while Uganda lies inland, both Kenya and Tanzania border the Indian Ocean. The coastal area of East Africa had been for centuries in contact with successive waves of foreigners notably the Arabs, the Indians, and the Portuguese—but it was not until the late 19th century that outside political influences began to seriously penetrate the interior of this region, which was comprised of geographically diverse arid and lush areas, and inhabited by a number of culturally distinct groups. As in the past, trade and exploration were the main pursuits. By the turn of the century, however, both Germany and Great Britain had established well-developed political interests and claims to the region; and plans were well underway for a modern railway system that would travel from the ancient city of Mombasa, on the Indian Ocean, to the shores of Lake Victoria and the wealthy African kingdom of Buganda.

Germany claimed the area south of a line just north of Mt. Kilimanjaro, which was called Tanganyika. Great Britain claimed the area just adjacent, stretching as far north as Somalia (then colonized by Italy). The need to build and administer the railroad led to the building of the city of Nairobi (conveniently located at a halfway point, and at the junction of the flat plains, where it was easy to build the roadbed, and the rich green highlands that could supply food) as well as the establishment of a colonial government.

After the First World War Tanganyika was ceded to Great Britain, and the whole territory under colonial government was often referred to as British East Africa (BEA). At the time of independence Tanganyika and the island of Zanzibar were consolidated to form the new nation of Tanzania. The boundary between Uganda and Kenya had been earlier drawn to facilitate Kenya's viability as an agriculturally based British colony (with significant numbers of permanent British settlers who planned to make their homes there). Resident aliens at the time of independence were given the opportunity to become Kenyan citizens. All three new nation states remained part of the British Commonwealth.

For some ten years following Independence in the early 1960's the three nations maintained a useful loose federation known as the East Africa Community. They shared administration of parts of the railroad, travel on Lake Victoria, common postal services, sharing of educational facilities at the University level and other features that were deemed to be of mutual economic interest. Political pressures caused this federation to break down in the mid-1970's, making national boundaries more salient than at any time in the past; since 1984, however, restrictions have decreased and it appears that a period of renewed cooperation is developing.

Overview of Linguistic Diversity as the Context for Swahili as a Regional Lingua Franca

Linguistically the boundaries dividing the three countries can be seen to be somewhat arbitrary. Along the borders there are often groups that share the same language and basic culture who are divided simply by a political boundary. This is especially true of the pastoral Maasai who occupy both sides of the Kenya-Tanzania border in the Serengeti plain. A similar situation exists along the northern part of the Kenya-Uganda border. At the time that boundary was drawn, major consideration was given to the important kingdom of Baganda which was located entirely within Uganda.

In all three countries the internal linguistic diversity is great. Though precise figures for the number of languages in each country are not available, there are approximately forty in Kenya, more than one hundred in Tanzania, and over thirty in Uganda. Four major African language families—Bantu, Nilo-Saharan, Cushitic, and Khoison—are represented in the overall territory. Tanzania's languages come from all four language families, but more than 90% are from the Bantu family. In Kenya there are Bantu languages (including Kikuyu, Kamba, Luyia, Swahili), Nilo-Saharan languages (all from the Nilotic group, including Oholuo, Maa, and Kalenjin), and Cushitic languages (occurring mostly in the northeastern part of the country and including Somali and Rendille). Among the inhabitants about two-thirds speak Bantu mother-tongues, while nearly one third speak Nilotic mother-tongues. Two major language families are represented in Uganda. Bantu languages (including most prominently Luganda) occur mostly in the southern part of the country, while Nilo-Saharan languages (mostly Nilotic such as Acholi and Lango, but including also Sudanic ones) are spoken in the north. This does not include, of course, the small pockets of languages imported from the Indian sub-continent with small groups of traders who began to settle in East Africa over the past hundred years.

Historically, none of these languages has assumed dominance in terms of numbers of speakers. Today, with more than fifty million people inhabiting this entire region of East Africa, no single language has more than five million mother-tongue speakers.

In this context there are a number of obvious features about Swahili that have played a role in its development as an historically important *lingua franca* within the region. First, it is a Bantu language. Most inhabitants of the region speak a Bantu language as mother tongue; another Bantu language is easier for them to learn than a language from another group. Secondly, Swahili is spoken indigenously along the coast. For centuries this has been the East African language of contact for traders approaching from the Indian Ocean. Thirdly, long before the 19th century the culture of the people who first spoke this language (also called the Swahili) was urban and literate, and had incorporated the Islamic religion.

This effectively meant that Swahili was more "developed" as a language, and more "open" to change and accommodation to cultural differences and innovations.

Brief History of the Swahili Language

The exact origin of the Swahili language is uncertain, but there are reports as early as the second century A.D. that there were indigenous urban trading settlements along the coast of the Indian Ocean, south of the horn of Africa. According to Whiteley (1969, p.31) "On present linguistic evidence . . . some form of Proto-Standard Swahili was being spoken on the coast before the tenth century." It seems likely that Swahili developed first in the north, in what is now Somalia, south of Mogadishu, near the Lamu archipelago and the Tana river estuary, and then spread south along the coast and off-shore islands.

When the island of Kilwa was visited by the Arabic traveller Ibn Batutu in 1332, he reported that there were native poets, who wrote lyric and epic poems in the Swahili language, using the Arabic script (Heine 1970). At that time Kilwa was the cultural center of the Zenj empire, which governed the coastal territory as far south as the Zambezi River and used Swahili as the *lingua franca*. As a major part of Arab and Persian influence, Islam seems to have become a part of the Swahili culture during the Zenji period, which spanned several centuries (from before the 10th century up to the late 15th century when Vasco da Gama appeared with his Portuguese fleet). This was a period of brisk competitive maritime trade among countries that accessed the Indian Ocean, particularly those that could use the monsoon trade winds to advantage. The Zenj "empire" itself seems to have consisted large-ly of a set of city-states like Lamu and Mombasa that were situated on small islands or along the coast where there were heavy man-grove swamps that could provide a deterrent to swift invasion from the sea. Very maneuverable single-masted sailing ships cal-led *dhows* were built from mangrove wood and used for most maritime transportation in the region. Together with more modern vessels dhows continue to be used today.

Exactly when and how the Swahili language and culture

emerged is not clear. Western scholars in the early 20th century, citing the heavy influence of Arabic on the language and the evidence of settlement, intermarriage, and the spread of Islam from Arabia, put forward the idea that Swahili was a "mixed language," based on Arabic and Bantu, possibly a creolized trade language of the Indian Ocean.

This hypothesis is no longer considered valid. The Arabs came as traders rather than settlers. When they have stayed on, the tendency has been to intermarry and to become quickly Swahilized. More importantly, there is no evidence within the language itself of creolization or reduced form. Swahili grammatical structure retains a fully elaborate Bantu morphology (including, for example, at least seven noun classes that are indicated by morphological prefixes, and that require concord with adjectives and subject and object markers within the verb), and its core vocabulary as well as its phonology is clearly Bantu. The only possible reduction is the lack of phonemic tone, which most other Bantu languages in East Africa do have. Moreover, even if this is a "loss" there is no need to postulate Arabic or foreign influence, as the surrounding non-Bantu languages from the region, such as Somali, are also non-tonal.

Arabic influence on the Swahili language seems limited almost entirely to the addition of literary genres and additions to the lexicon. Although some studies suggest that as much as 35% of the lexicon may be borrowed from other languages, mostly from Arabic, estimates go as high as 70% for the proportion of these borrowings that are related to Islam or Islamic education. Arabic is still taught in *madrassas* (Islamic primary schools) along the coast, though it is used now almost exclusively to study the Koran and religious documents.

It seems likely that in earlier times, among some of the population there existed a Swahili-Arabic bilingualism of a diglossic nature, with Arabic being used to discuss semantic domains such as theology, jurisprudence, rhetoric, and medieval science. This facilitated lexical borrowing for exactly those areas that were not part of the indigenous culture. Traditional semantic domains and genres were less 'kely to borrow new words. For example, the indigenous societ has strong associations with the sea. As we might thus expect, vocabulary dealing with the sea is largely Bantu and comprises a significant portion of the Swahili lexicon; further, some of the best proverbs (a traditional genre) are associated with the sea.

Swahili was used as a language of trade not only along the coast, but also when caravans were formed to go into the interior in search of ivory, animal skins, and, for a time, slaves. Most of these caravans went through the area that is now Tanzania, through land occupied by other Bantu-speaking groups. In Kenya the caravans had to traverse through territory occupied by the Maasai, who were Nilotic-speaking, and who were known for their fierce warriors. Swahili was less useful in negotiating with this group.

As a *lingua franca* over a period of several centuries Swahili has often been in a situation of diglossia, spoken by individuals who spoke Swahili in particular semantic or social domains, and who spoke at least one other language in other domains. This has led to continued borrowing into Swahili where new areas were introduced. A portion of the vocabulary for card playing, for example, is borrowed from Portuguese, reflecting the period of introduction. In recent years, many new words have been borrowed from English. Many terms for plants and animals have been taken from other African languages. All this has given the language a property of adaptability and elasticity which more culturally isolated languages do not have.

Colonial Influences On Regional Patterns of Language Use

The influences of the British and Germans began in the 19th century when their interest in trade and geographical exploration led them to go beyond the coastal region into the interior. This expansion of trade accelerated the spread of Swahili along these trade routes.

This spread was, however, not uniform throughout the region. Because Zanzibar had by this time become the major focus for trade (rather than ports further north) and because the routes through Tanganyika were less hazardous than those through the more northern Maasai-occupied land, the spread of Swahili during this early period was far more significant in Tanganyika than in Kenya or Uganda. In fact, because of the necessity to negotiate with the Maasai, caravans that took the northern route often brought interpreters who could speak Maa rather than rely on Swahili.

Trade and exploration also opened the region to missionaries who came in large numbers to spread Christianity, and the kingdom of Baganda became an early stronghold. Missionary interest was probably enhanced by the presence or recent presence of the slave trade. The British Royal Navy negotiated a protective treaty with Seyyid Said, the Sultan of Zanzibar, in exchange for his help in putting down the slave trade in the early 1800's.

Though the language policies of the British and the Germans differed, at first neither group made much effort to introduce English or German, or to in anyway change local patterns of language use. Much as they had done in India, the British administrators and missionary teachers set about learning the local languages as needed. In Tanganyika, under German control, interest in learning the indigenous languages was particularly strong. As the Christian missions penetrated into areas away from the trade routes (which was more likely in the British controlled territory) they found that Swahili was less well known. However, as colonial interests and involvements became stronger it became clear that there was a need to provide organization and administration across tribal boundaries and that policies would have to be set that would dictate the usage of local languages and *lingua francas*.

These language policies, based largely on the simple need to facilitate communication, had the most direct influence on changing regional patterns of language use. They involved basically two realms: organization and administration, and education.

Education in British territory was almost exclusively the province of the missionaries. Most of them favored the use of the local mother-tongues for teaching and translating the Bible. Their feeling was that the mother-tongue would be most likely to capture the spirituality of the Biblical teachings. Though this was to some extent an impractical decision because of the number of different languages involved, they felt that Swahili was not a viable solution because of its long association with the Islamic religion. In Uganda and the western part of the territory there was also some negative association of Swahili with slave-trading.

In fact, when the United Missionary Conference was held in Nairobi in 1909 there was a debate over whether Swahili or English should become the *lingua franca* in which it was decided that English should become the lingua franca. The vernacular or mother-tongue was to be used for the first four years of school, with English being used after that. Swahili was still to be taught as a subject and used as a medium of instruction in some schools such as those in Nairobi. Educational policy thus did not assign much prestige or utility to Swahili in parts of the territory where it was not already widely used.

In Tanganyika, under German control, educational policy took a different turn. At first some schools tried to provide primary instruction in German, but when this produced almost uniform failure it was quickly given up. Because there were so many different language groups in Tanganyika, and perhaps also because the major urban concentration was along the coast in or around Dar es Salaam where Swahili was the mother-tongue, the decision was made to use Swahili in educational institutions.

This decision meant that books and teaching materials had to be prepared. Since the late 19th century, missionaries and other interested foreigners had begun to transliterate Swahili into Roman script and to systematize their knowledge of the language so that it could be taught to others. Though the indigenous Swahili culture was a literate one, this literacy was based exclusively on Swahili written in Arabic script. Roman scripted Swahili was being newly introduced, and met with considerable success. In 1914 the German Protestant Mission published its newspaper *Pwani-na-Bara* in Swahili with a circulation of about 2000.

Language policy with respect to organization and adminstration was less dissimilar between the two colonial powers. In building the railroads, both quickly adopted Swahili as the *lingua franca*. As administrative needs increased, Swahili continued to be used more and more.

However, in British controlled territory there were several large ethnolinguistic groups—notably the Ganda, the Luo, the

Luyia, the Kikuyu, and the Kamba—whose languages were used at the district level. In contrast, in Tanganyika administrative political boundaries were such that a single local language was rarely available to be used. Further, the Germans took a greater interest in training local people to do administration and set their educational policy in accordance with this need. Thus in Tanganyika Swahili quickly became known as both the language of learning and government employment, and acquired considerable prestige.

Another factor which no doubt played a role in the differing evolving roles for Swahili was that while the Germans maintained their administrative center in Dar es Salaam on the Swahili coast, the British soon moved their administrative center from coastal Mombasa to the more centrally located Nairobi, amongst the Kikuyu, the Maasai, and the Kamba. Swahili continued to develop as an important lingua franca, but in the absence of a local group who spoke it as a first language it began to assume the character of a sub-standard dialect, "up-country" Swahili.

In 1920 Kenya and Uganda became crown colonies of Great Britain and Tanganyika came under British control as well. During the 1920's there was a temporary convergence of educational policies in Kenya, Tanzania, and Uganda, in which the British accorded Swahili more prominence than in the past, but this did not last.

In Tanganyika the British built on the German administrative and educational structure, but after they took over English was introduced in key domains and there was a resulting loss of prestige by Swahili. In primary schools Swahili was still used as the medium of instruction, but for secondary schools it was English. Though the language of the lower courts was Swahili, the language of the higher courts was English. Newspapers continued to be published in Swahili, but the new, and therefore prestigious, media of glossy magazines and films were in English (or occasionally other foreign languages).

In Kenya, after the British takeover of Tanganyika, an effort was made to use more Swahili in certain areas, especially administratively. However, schools continued to be left largely in the hands of the missionaries, and the medium of instruction continued to be either mother-tongue or English. English was becoming more important in Kenya as Great Britain had made a decision to colonize there and had offered tracts of arable land to European settlers, especially British veterans of the First World War. Important political and administrative posts were thus held by the British, and it was not foreseen that this would change significantly in future years.

Swahili made inroads in particular areas. For example, it was made the language of the East African territorial army called the *King's African Rifles* and of the security forces. Further, trainees were sent from all parts of British East Africa to work in other areas. This promoted a tremendous regional identification, especially among the classes who contributed to these forces.

Also important was the fact that after World War I Tanganyika and the Swahili-speaking island of Zanzibar just off its coast had come under control of the same colonial power. With Great Britain governing all of East Africa the idea of standardizing Swahili became practicable. In 1925 an education conference held in Dar es Salaam led to proposals for standardized spelling and the establishment of a Central Publishing Committee. In 1927, following the recommendation of the British Governor, Swahili was designated one of Uganda's official languages, giving it equal status with Luganda. Early the following year, 1928, the dialect of Zanzibar was officially adopted as the standard dialect of East Africa at an inter-territorial conference held in Mombasa.

Regional convergence on the use of Swahili proved to be short-lived, however. Swahili's status as an official language in Uganda lasted only a year. The politically powerful Ganda mis-trusted its rivalry with Luganda, the missionaries worried that it was Islamic in character, and some educators felt that it would retard modernization.

In Kenya Swahili speakers all used a dialect somewhat different from the Zanzibar dialect that had become the selected standard. The coastal speakers did not fully accept the Zanzibar standard (see,e.g., Khalid 1977), and disapproved of the up-country dialect that was growing in proportion to the urbanization that was taking place in the center of the country. At some distance from the coastal mother-tongue speakers, this growth sector for Swahili was little influenced by the Swahili people and was used in formal contexts such as programs by the Kenya Broadcasting Corporation as well as for informal everyday encounters.

All this gave the use of Swahili in Kenya a different character and a different base than that in Tanganyika and Zanzibar. Whiteley's (1969) observation was that "if Swahili was the language of the country in Tanganyika, in Kenya it was the language of the towns, especially Nairobi, where people from all parts of the country found it a convenient bulwark against the loneliness of city life as well as a ready tool to exploit the attractions the city offered" (p. 67).

In the 1950's there were more Swahili newspapers published in Nairobi than in Dar es Salaam, but a sense of competition with mother-tongue languages was more keenly felt in somewhat the same way it was in Uganda. In Tanganyika, for example, the political party TANU adopted the use of Swahili with no problem. In Kenya, shortly before independence, the political party KANU initially proposed using Swahili all over the country and produced their party newspaper in it; at a later date, however, Luo, Kikuyu, and Kamba were also used.

By the close of the colonial era, English as well as Swahili had grown in stature. There was first of all its continued importance in international trade and in negotiating (notwithstanding the violence of the "emergency" period) political independence with Great Britain. In addition, universities had been set up where English was (and still is) the exclusive medium of instruction: Makarere University in Kampala, Uganda, the University of Dar es Salaam in Tanganyika, and the University of Nairobi in Kenya. The newly emerging African intellectuals were anxious to communicate with Africans outside the East African region and with the international intellectual community. East African authors such as James Ngugi (later to write under the name Ngugi wa Thiong'o) began to use the literary genre of the novel, written in English.

National Policies on Language Use

As with language policies during the colonial period the major two areas in which policy has been legislated concern political administration and education. As mass media has become more and more important, policy regarding dissemination of information through these channels has become another important area of language policy as well.

The first president of Tanzania, Julius Nyerere, actively encouraged the use of Swahili in all walks of life, including all spheres of government and politics. It is thus the "official" language as well as the national language. In education Swahili is used as the medium of instruction all through elementary school, and English medium schools are not introduced until the secondary and tertiary levels. English maintains some status as co-official language, as it is also used at higher levels of government, especially in the judiciary and in dealing with international affairs. The print media of newspapers and magazines utilizes both Swahili and English, as does radio broadcasting. However, more Swahili is used, especially in broadcasting and other oral media. Another important government policy has been to set up a National Swahili Council which acts much like an academy of language, passing on any new publications and working to standardize the modernization of the language through the borrowing of needed terms and expressions.

In Kenya Swahili was proclaimed the national language as well, but this did not mean that it was to displace other languages in all affairs of national interest. A small committee of musicians, some British and some African, were commissioned to compose a national anthem with Swahili lyrics and an indigenous East African tune (which turned out to be a lullaby). Swahili continued as the language of the military. Swear-in ceremonies of government officials were to be carried out in Swahili only. But English was to be the "official" language, making it the language of Parliament and offices of national government. In 1974 Kenya's first president Jomo Kenyatta proclaimed that Swahili should also be used in the Parliament. Since that time Members of Parliament have been required to know both Swahili and English in order to participate fully in debate. Monetary currency is marked in both Swahili and English.

With regard to education a Kenya Education Commission was set up in 1964 to study the situation and make recommendations for carrying out the educational needs of the country. The resulting report, often referred to as the Ominde report (so—called for the Chairman of the Commission) recommended that mother-tongues (and in linguistically mixed areas occasionally Swahili) be used for the first three standards, with Swahili and English taught as subjects, and that schools be English medium from standard four onwards, with Swahili continuing throughout the seven year curriculum as a required subject. Secondary and tertiatary education was to continue as English medium. In 1984 significant changes were made, introducing the "8–4–4" system. Elementary education was extended to eight standards with a shift in emphasis in curriculum, and with Swahili being tested at the end of this period, which was not previously emphasized. Additionally, though the secondary schools continue to use English as medium, Swahili has now been made a compulsory subject.

Print media is largely in English and Swahili. Television broadcasting is done only in English and Swahili, with the news being delivered in both languages at different times of day. On the radio there are local broadcasts in some of the mother tongues, including Kikuyu, Kamba, Luyia, Luo, and Somali. Among some of the pastoral groups radio is a far more effective media than television or any of the print media. Broadcasting media are government controlled, whereas print media is not.

National efforts to research and develop the Swahili language have been undertaken, though they do not match the level of investment made by the Tanzanian government. In 1971 the University of Nairobi launched a Department of Linguistics and African Languages in which Swahili is taught. The National Council for Science and Technology has requested the preparation of an English-Swahili medical dictionary, which should be available by 1987. However, so far nothing approximating the institute of Swahili research discussed in the 1979–1983 National Five Year Plan has come about.

In Uganda it has never been possible to agree to the use of a single African language as *the* national language. Luganda, language of the historically politically powerful Ganda group, has long been used as a regional *lingua franca* and was designated one of six nationally recognized languages to be used in public education (along with Ateso/Akarimojong, Lugbara, Lwo (sometimes

referred to as Dholuo), Runyankore/Rukiga, and Runyoro/
Ruturo). Since the introduction of Swahili through traders and by
the British organization of the King's African Rifles and the territorial security forces, it has served as an important *lingua franca* in
other areas. However, its association with the military—in particular with the generally less educated classes from which these forces
were drawn—and the fact that Swahili is not a mother-tongue for
any Ugandan group, has meant that it does not connote positive
national identity. English has continued to play an important role
both in government and in education. English probably enjoys a
more secure status as *lingua franca* in Uganda than in either Kenya
or Tanzania.

The Current Status of Swahili in East Africa

Swahili is widely spoken today throughout East Africa. In
addition to having been designated the national language of both
Kenya and Tanzania, and being promulgated as a regional language in Uganda, it is also used in parts of Zaire and Rwanda and
Burundi. As the political situation in Uganda has been extremely
unstable and is only now (1986) beginning to be resolved, the
policies there may change.

Swahili spread from the coastal area into the interior of East
Africa through its use as a *lingua franca* in trade. It has continued to
be the language of retail trade and commerce, especially in urban
areas between people from different tribal backgrounds.
Additionally, it was used early on to facilitate administrative
undertakings, such as the building of railroads, and the organization of services at a non-local level. These are instances of what
Mazrui (1975) has called the organizational impetus for the spread
of a *lingua franca*. This would seem to account for most of the initial
spread of Swahili in the region. Once a language has been spread
to a certain level, however, it becomes available for purposes other
than those which may have initiated the spread. For example, the
organizational potential of Swahili was exercised by the indigenous population in the Maji Rebellion of 1909, in which Tanganyi-
kans rallied in a last military effort to oust the Germans.

Further, the fact of there being a language that is spoken beyond the bounds of one's mother tongue can give individuals a sense of belonging to a unit larger than the local political unit. This can lead to what Mazrui has called the inspirational thrust of a *lingua franca*, whereby people are motivated to learn and use a language in order to identify with what it stands for.

This inspirational thrust in the spread of Swahili did not take place until this century, and it occurred first in Tanzania where it was spoken longer by a more widely spread populace who had quickly grasped its organizational value. Often cited is the example of the five Chagga tribes, each with their own distinct dialect, who decided, in order to communicate equitably amongst themselves, to adopt Swahili as their *lingua franca* (Scotton 1978). Because of the German language policies (to use Swahili as the medium of instruction as much as possible) Swahili had become closely associated with learning and education, and with economic opportunity through government employment as well as trade. Though it lost considerable prestige during the British colonial period, since independence and President Nyerere's policy of using Swahili throughout the government as well as in other spheres of life it has regained much of its previous level of prestige.

In Kenya Swahili is now often seen as symbolic of Africanness in contrast with English, which connotes to many too much of a cultural identification with the colonial period. At the same time, though, for some citizens, mostly from non-Bantu groups, Swahili is seen as more symbolic of Bantu identity than of national or regional identity, and there is resistance to being culturally assimilated. In addition, many see the continued organizational value of English for higher education, modern technology, and international trade and communication. As Kenya, in contrast to Tanzania, has pursued a capitalistic as well as democratic program for national development, this last point has high salience for Kenya's role as a major center for international exchange (including, for example, being host country to the United Nations and several other donors that serve all of East and Southern Africa).

In Uganda Swahili continues to be seen as organizationally

useful, but does not seem to have any value yet for forging national identity. In fact its potential for regional unification within East Africa is sometimes seen as antithetical to Ugandan national interests.

It is possible to see these contrasts as a kind of progressive development, with the continuing growth of Swahili being driven by both organizational and inspirational associations in Tanzania, by some organizational and some inspirational associations in Kenya, and by primarily organizational associations in Uganda.

In all three countries there is unstable multilingualism based on rapid social change—reflecting both the changing needs of the societies and the changing linguistic repertoires of individuals (including here, especially, education and literacy levels, and exposure to other languages). As Swahili acquires more speakers, and urbanization increases (as a result of both economic development and population pressures), certain interpersonal domains of usage are opened to Swahili—mother-tongue (and occasionally English) bilingualism, while other more formal and official domains of usage are opened to Swahili-English bilingualism. In association with this there is a certain amount of "language mixing" or code-switching within the sentence unit. There does not seem any likelihood of Swahili and English forming anything like a new pidgin or creole, although, among certain age cohorts (around the teenage years of secondary school end early university education) in Nairobi, there is a fairly well-developed kind of slang called *Sheng*, which is used as a kind of age-specific "secret" language, and which clearly involves a mixing of English and occasionally other foreign words into the basic Swahili syntax.

In Kenya especially, where economic development is taking place most rapidly, both Swahili and English seem to be acquiring speakers. Impressionistically, there seems to be a tendency for what might be thought of as *"dimodal diglossia"* for many speakers in some domains, whereby English is more preferred for reading and especially writing, while Swahili is more preferred for oral communication. This does not seem to be a straightforward official-unofficial or formal-informal splitting. For example, broadcasts and public speeches are increasingly presented in Swahili, while bilinguals often seem to prefer English language newspapers.

The aesthetic and formally expressive uses of languages present a more complex situation, especially since mother-tongue literacy is fairly recent and since many of the traditional Swahili literary genres—those that were associated with the Arabic script and the Islamic religion—were not adopted with the general spread of Swahili as a *lingua franca*. Many creative literary genres were basically adopted along with the acquisition of English, but since independence these are often questioned, altered, and even abandoned (see p'Bitek 1973, Gachukia 1986, Wanjala 1981). For example, intellectual concern over producing Kenyan literature in English and western European language genres has led to the important inclusion of oral literature in the university curriculum and the writing of some works in mother-tongues. In Kenya, following the lead of Tanzania, literature in the creative genres of novels, stories, and poetry is now being written by both native and non-native speakers.

It is now scarcely a generation since Kenya, Tanzania, and Uganda became independent nations. The situation is highly complex and changing. Nevertheless, we speculate in concurrence with the recent statement by Abdulaziz (1985): "For the foreseeable future, Swahili is likely to gain ground all the time as it emerges as a true national *lingua franca* of the three East African countries. English, for a long time, will have a secure established place as the language of education and international communication. In Uganda and Kenya the mother tongues may receive more attention but they are unlikely to develop functions outside intra-ethnic communication."

Notes

1. For much of the historical discussion a synthesis has been drawn from several of the works listed in the bibliography that are not individually cited.

2. Since this paper was written (February 1986) both the authors have attended a conference on English in East Africa, and Abdulaziz has also attended a conference on Standardization of African languages and on scientific and technical terminology within the region. These recent discussions with other

colleagues have corroborated the basic ideas presented in this paper, and also have indicated that, perhaps because Swahili is an indigenously African language, there is an increasingly lively interest in its spread and development.

References

Abdulaziz, M.H. 1971. Tanzania's National Language Policy and the Rise of a Swahili Political Culture. In: W.H. Whiteley, ed. *Language Use and Social Change*. London: Oxford University Press, 160–178.

Abdulaziz Mikilifi, M.H. 1972. Triglossia and Swahili-English Bilingualism in Tanzania. *Language in Society* 1, 197–213.

Abdulaziz, Mohamed H. 1979. *Muyaka: 19th Century Swahili Popular Poetry.* Nairobi: Kenya Literature Bureau.

Abdulaziz, Mohamed H. 1987a. A Sociolinguistic Profile of East Africa. In: U. Ammon, N. Dittmar, K. Mattheier, eds. *Handbook "Sociolinguistics"*, Berlin, New York: De Gruyter.

Abdulaziz, Mohammad H. 1987b. Language and Social Change. In: *A General History of Africa: Vol. VIII, Africa since 1935.* UNESCO.

p'Bitek, Okot. 1973. *Africa's Cultural Revolution.* Nairobi: MacMillan Books for Africa.

Chilipaine, F.A. and J.A.C. Mapanji 1985. *Report of the Organizing Conference of the Linguistic Association for Southern Africa Development Coordinating Conference Universities.* Zomba: University of Malawi.

Eastman, Carol M. 1983. *Language Planning, An Introduction.* San Francisco: Chandler and Sharp Publishers, Inc.

Fishman, Joshua A. 1969. National Languages and Languages of Wider Communication in the Developing Nations. *Anthropological Linguistics* 111–135.

Gachukia, Eddah. 1986. Language and the African Writer. Faculty Seminar paper for Dept. of Literature, University of Nairobi.

Gorman, T.P. ed. 1970. *Language in Education in Eastern Africa.* Nairobi: Oxford University Press.

Heine, Bernd. 1970. *Status and Use of African Lingua Francas.* München: Weltforum Verlag.

Khalid, Abdallah. 1977. *The Liberation of Swahili.* Nairobi: East African Literature Bureau.

Ladefoged, Peter, Ruth Glick, Clive Criper, eds. 1971. *Language in Uganda.* Nairobi: Oxford University Press.

Mazrui, Ali A. 1967. The National Language Question in East Africa. *East Africa Journal*, June.

Mazrui, Ali A. 1975. *The Political Sociology of the English Language: An African Perspective.* The Hague: Mouton.

Miller, Charles. 1971. *The Lunatic Express.* New York: Ballantine Press.

Mosha, M. 1971. The National Language Question in Uganda. *Journal of East African Languages.*

Parkin, D.J. 1974. Language Switching in Nairobi. In: W.H. Whiteley, ed. *Language in Kenya*. Nairobi: Oxford University Press.

Polome, E.C. and C.P. Hill eds. 1980. *Language in Tanzania*. London: Oxford University Press.

Republic of Kenya. *1979–1983 Development Plan, Part I*. Nairobi: Government of Kenya.

Scotton, Carol Meyrs. 1971. *Choosing a Lingua Franca in an African Capital*. Edmonton, Alberta: Linguistic Research Inc.

Scotton, Carol Myers. 1978. Language in East Africa: Linguistic Patterns and Political Ideologies. In: J.A. Fishman, ed. *Advances in the Study of Societal Multilingualism*. The Hague: Mouton.

Spear, Thomas and Derek Nurse. 1985. *The Swahili*. Philadelphia: University of Pennsylvania Press.

Wanjala, C. 1981. The Growth of a Literary Tradition in East Africa. *Journal of Eastern African Research and Development II*.

Whiteley, Wilfred. 1969. *Swahili: The Rise of a National Language*. London: Methuen.

Whiteley, Wilfred. ed. 1971. *Language Use and Social Change: Problems of Multilingualism with Special Reference to Eastern Africa*. London: Oxford University Press.

Whiteley, Wilfred. ed. 1974. *Language in Kenya*. London: Oxford University Press.

Implementing Morocco's Arabization Policy: Two Problems of Classification*

Beverley Seckinger

Introduction

From 1912–1956, Morocco was governed as a French Protectorate. During those years, the French established an administrative network of government ministries and bureaus, a system of secular schools, banks, telephones, post offices, roads, and railways. All of these structures officially operated primarily, if not exclusively, in French. Following independence from France in 1956, the Moroccan constitutions (of 1962, 1970, and 1972) declared the kingdom a "sovereign Muslim state, whose official language is Arabic." To get from such a declaration ("selection of norm," to use Haugen's (1983) terminology) to its "codification," "elaboration" and "implementation," successive policies of "Arabization" have been devised and legislated, with the aim of ultimately converting those French-run domains into Arabic ones.

The discussion that follows suggests two kinds of problems with the ways in which Morocco's language situation has been described and analyzed, and with the policies that have been formulated to reshape that situation: First, models of language use

68

which treat the oral and written language varieties used in Morocco as distinct codes/systems—i.e., in context X, speakers use language Y (*or* language Z)—are inaccurate idealizations of how language distribution "ought" to look, and inadequate to capture the high degree of code-switching and -mixing that characterizes much of language use in Morocco. Second, implementing Arabization policy is a slow, uneven process. In the course of the changeover from one system of language use to another—a change officially considered to be for the (eventual) good of Moroccan society—a great many individuals unfortunately fall between the cracks created by these changing systems. Either they are trained in one language, then expected to work in another, or they are partially trained in one language, then expected to continue their training in another, without sufficient preparation. Both problems stem from a gap between tidy theory and an untidy world, where languages can't be classed into separate boxes, nor peoples' use of them be guided into restricted paths. Both problems have important implications for planners and policy makers, who must accurately assess situations before acting to change them.

After a brief description of the languages of Morocco, and the kinds of sociolinguistic statements about their distribution which are commonly made (see Boukous, 1979a and 1979b, Moatassime, 1974, Abou-Abou, 1984), the course of post Protectorate (1956-present) Moroccan language policy is outlined. These discussions are followed by a series of ethnographic observations, offered to illuminate some of the gaps between typical sociolinguistic profiles of Morocco and the normative policies which reflect them, and actual language use in several contexts.

The Languages of Morocco

Berber

Estimates of the number of native Berber-speakers in Morocco range from 40% to as high as 60% of the population (for example, see Moatassime, 1974, p. 641). Many rural-dwelling Arabic-speakers, too, acquire some familiarity with Berber through contact with their neighbors and schoolmates. Three major dialects are usually identified (Tarifiyt, Tamazight, and Tashelhit),[1] each characterized by much internal variation, not only from region to region, but from village to village, and even from one hillside to the next. Many of these varieties, particularly at the far ends of the geographical spectrum, are not mutually intelligible, so that Berbers from different dialect areas usually communicate with each other in Moroccan Arabic (Gravel, 1979: 78).

Arabic

The dialect here termed "Moroccan Arabic" is also characterized by internal variation. Gravel speaks of an "urban variety" that traces its origins to the language of the first Arab conquerors in the late seventh century and, later, to the colloquial speech of the Spanish-Arab refugees (moriscos), and of a "rural variety . . . brought into Morocco during the nomadic invasions of the Beni Hilal Arabs in the twelfth century" (1979: 92). Boukous distinguishes three types of Moroccan Arabic, "according to the ethnic origins of their speakers" (1979a: 18) which he terms "city Arabic," "mountain Arabic," and "Bedouin Arabic." Heath (1983) writes of "a considerable range" of Moroccan (Colloquial) Arabic dialects, split up along geographical-regional, urban/rural, Muslim/Jewish, adult/child, male/female, and elegant/vulgar lines. Despite such variation, though, and despite the fact that it is often possible to identify a speaker on the basis of what Heath calls "telltale indicators" (of geographical and social information—phonological, morphological, and lexical), these various sub-dialects are essentially mutually comprehensible, and will hereafter be referred to collectively as Moroccan Arabic (MA).

Classical Arabic, the language of the Qur'an and of Classical poetry, is still used in religious and traditional literary contexts, while Modern Standard Arabic, an updated/ing version of the Classical language (see below) is used for television newscasts, newspapers and magazines, modern literature, descriptions and instructions printed on packaged products, etc. The functional range of Modern Standard Arabic is being expanded in the course of its modernization and standardization. Because, for the purposes of this paper, the important contrast is not between these two varieties, but rather between both of them, on the one hand,

and MA on the other, both Classical and Modern Standard Arabic will henceforth be referred to under the common rubric of Standard Arabic (SA). Although the grammatical categories of SA and MA are generally similar or even identical, and MA vocabulary retains numerous SA cognates, the two forms of Arabic may be described as "distinct languages with many differences in segmental phonology, canonical-shape norms, and morpheme structure" (Heath, 1983: 63), as well as in syntax and lexicon. For detailed discussions of the structural differences between SA and MA, see Heath, 1983, or Abbasi, 1977.

In spite of its use as a national *lingua franca* across a broad range of contexts,[2] and the fact that it is natively acquired, while SA is not, MA has never been seriously considered in policy decisions. "Because of its close relationship with the Qur'an," SA is regarded as "divine and sacred . . . *the* correct form of Arabic and the one form of it for people to learn" (Abbasi, 1977: 90).[3] In an attitudinal survey of Arabic-French bilinguals in Fes, SA ("Classical Arabic") was overwhelmingly judged the "richest" and "most beautiful" of the languages used in Morocco (Bentahila, 1983). On a similar questionnaire presented to students and literate professionals in Casablanca, virtually all respondants chose SA as the language they "would like to see adopted in schools" (Abbasi, 1977: 183), citing its "purity/standardization," "linguistic superiority," "historical legacy," and its political "necessity" as a step toward pan-Arab unity, as the primary reasons for their choice. Conversely, MA was regarded as "impure," "aesthetically and expressively inferior," a "deformation of language," and therefore "should not, according to 94% of the participants, be a language of education and literacy" (Abbasi, 1977, 188, 230). This type of reasoning seems to be widely accepted by the lay public, as well as by professional and policymaking groups in Morocco, and therefore SA has always been the variety to be officially planned for and legislated.

European Languages

Of the European languages used in Morocco, French is still by far the most influential. As the linguistic legacy of the 44-year Protectorate period, French remains an important language of administration, education, technology, tourism, television, and conversation in diverse contexts. Spanish, leftover from a longer but less pervasive colonialism (see Abbasi, 1977,) can still be found in the cities of the north, and has left its mark particularly on some of the northern sub-dialects of Moroccan Arabic. Finally, English—perhaps as an alternative to the lingering, post-colonial bad taste of French, but also due to the spread of computer technology, American products, British and American music, and increasing numbers of English-speaking tourists, as well as many other factors—is steadily growing in use, popularity, and, for some, a certain chic-ness.[4]

Language and National Identity

In addition to their communicative functions, each of these languages plays a distinct role in the construction of Moroccan social reality and the shaping of Moroccan national identity (see, for example, Gallagher, 1964, Moatassime, 1974, or Hamzaoui, 1976). The indigenous language before the Arab conquest of the late seventh century, Berber has had the longest history of any of these languages within Morocco. But while things Berber—songs, dances, traditional arts and dress—are often ceremoniously displayed as living (and lucrative) symbols of Morocco's "cultural heritage" (one glitzy example of which is Marrakech's annual *Festival national des arts populaires*), the Berber language has been scrupulously ignored by official language policy. If Berber "traditions" are on the one hand a source of national pride (and income), Berber-ness also stands for backwardness to many of those most anxious to urbanize and "modernize" Morocco. The Berber language may be considered suitable for singing folk songs, but policymakers apparently do not find it an appropriate medium for news broadcasts, classroom study, or publication (the works of Ahmed Boukous provide interesting discussions of a variety of attempts to extend the use of Berber into these areas).

By contrast, French represents technological, economic, and even "cultural" development (that is, the dubious "progress" of Westernization) for many Moroccans, and is frequently flaunted as a badge of "modernity." As noted above, French is still spoken and written in a number of contexts, but attempts are being made to replace it with SA in the course of Arabization (see below). Other European languages function in similar ways, if to lesser extents, since considerably fewer Moroccans speak or write them fluently.

Standard Arabic is both a symbol and a vehicle for not only pan-Arab and Islamic unity, but Moroccan unity as well; its high esteem is unparalleled among the great majority of Moroccans, regardless of their SA fluency (see Abbasi, 1977, or Ferguson, 1959b). Although Moroccan Arabic has no official national status, the percentage of MA speakers continues to rise as a result of urbanization and mass transportation and communication. And while SA is a unifying language at the pan-Arab level, MA identifies speakers both regionally as *Maghrebins* (along with Algerians and Tunisians), and locally as Moroccans. Nevertheless, official policy has been to de-emphasize natively acquired MA and Berber in favor of already-standardized languages with well-established written traditions. It is clear from King Hassan's 1964 speech at the National Conference on Education that Moroccan language policy is conceived of in the framework of international politics: "If we make our children citizens living in a Muslim country but also children equipped to live in a great ensemble speaking French and English, we will be armed to face our difficulties and our choices . . . prepar(ing) us to be citizens of our country, of the African continent, and of the world" (cited in Gallagher, 1964: 149).

Toward a Sociolinguistic Profile of Morocco

By examining the 1981 Moroccan census figures, along with the discussions of Gravel, Boukous, Abbasi, and Heath drawn on above, a rough sociolinguistic profile of Morocco can begin to be sketched from which the following types of statements might be made:

1. Berber and Moroccan Arabic are the only natively-acquired languages (aside from the tiny fraction of the population who are native French-speakers).
2. Standard Arabic and French are the only commonly written

languages, and as such are in what Boukous (1979a) calls a "state of competition," sharing a number of "functions" and "domains of usage" (although functional overlap is not complete).

3. Moroccan Arabic and Standard Arabic are in a diglossic relationship, although there is more functional overlap than Ferguson's (1959a) original model of functional complementarity might seem to imply (see below).

4. Moroccan Arabic is used as the national (oral) *lingua franca*, spoken by 75–90% of the Moroccan population.

5. If Berber-speakers want to communicate with anyone outside the limited area where their variety is spoken, they are forced to become multilingual, which usually means learning Moroccan Arabic.

6. Those least likely to speak Moroccan Arabic are rural Berber women who have little or no contact with those outside of their localities. Not surprisingly, this is also the group least likely to be involved in the public educational system. In 1982, only 13.2% of rural, school-aged (7–13) girls were enrolled in school, and fewer than 5% of rural females were literate (according to the 1981 census).

7. MA/Berber bilingualism, in varying degrees, is relatively common, though statistically undocumented (the 1981 census did not include a listing of Berber-speakers).[5]

Such statements, however useful, do not provide a complete profile of language distribution in Morocco. Treating "languages"[6] as separate, bounded (and labelled) codes, obscures the several types and degrees of code-switching and -mixing that are part of a full characterization of Moroccan language use.[7]

In a systematic study of foreign and diglossic mixing in Moroccan Arabic, Jeffrey Heath defines *code-switching* as "a pattern of textual production in which a speaker alternates between continuous utterance segments in one language Lx and another language Ly with abrupt and clearcut switching points, often at phrasal or clausal boundaries" (Heath, 1983: 37). *Borrowing* refers to "the adaptation of a lexical item Py from Ly into Lx becoming Px (that is, a regular lexical item in Lx satisfying phonological,

canonical-shape, and morphological rules for this language)"
(Heath, 1983: 37). Heath then goes on to discuss the problematic
nature of this idealized distinction, which is more accurately gra-
dient than neatly binary. Following Heath, the discussion below
uses *code-switching* to refer to switches between utterances, at
either the phrasal or lexical level, in which the two codes
(génerally) do not affect each other. For example:

Wahed nuba kunt	ana w Thami,	on s'est arrêté
One time	*Thami and I,*	*(we) stopped*
juste au feu rouge,	on parlait	kunna bRina n msiw
right at the spotlight,	*we were talking,*	*we were going to go*

lmra:ks.
to Marrakesh.   (cited in Bentahila, 1983: 36).

Code-mixing subsumes Heath's *borrowing,* as well as
not-quite-borrowed (that is, not-quite-fully morphologically
adapted) forms like /ma-ta-y-t-?utiliza-w-s/, cited in Heath as a
"spontaneous adaptation of Fr. *utiliser* retaining the Fr. vowels and
Fr. canonical shape of the stem, but with an entirely (MA) affixal
frame" (Heath, 1983: 39).

The discussion below is primarily concerned with MA/SA and
MA/Fr. switching and mixing, although instances of Berber/SA,
Berber/MA, and Berber/Fr. switching and mixing have been infor-
mally observed but not yet systematically studied. Common examples of MA/SA switching and mixing may be found by examining
Moroccan sportscasts, panel discussions, political interviews, and
discussions of "academic, political, commercial, or Islamic" topics,
where "a considerable admixture of CA (SA) stems and short
phrases" may be found (Heath, 1983: 40. See section 4.3 for examples of MA/SA texts.). MA/Fr. varieties are "relatively common"
among those "educated in schools where French was used as an
important medium of instruction," as well as among others who
have worked in France or Belgium, or in French-speaking contexts
in Morocco, e.g. banking, trade, tourism, and other bureaucratic or
commercial settings. The "typical pattern" found by Heath has

been for MA "to be the basic language with French phrases inserted from time to time"—most commonly NPs, but including also PPs, adjectives, adverbials and conjunctions, and French verbs inserted into MA morphological frames (see Heath, 1983, chapter 4, Bentahila, 1983, or Abbasi, 1977, for examples).

On the individual level, this means that a speaker's communicative competence (see Hymes, 1971, 1974) may include the ability to mix "Arabic and French parts of speech within the same speech event, the same sentence, or the same segment of talk" (Abbasi, 1977: 147).[8] An individual's expressive competence my include a wide range of mixed registers, the choice of which on a given occasion will be sensitive to a complex of social factors.[9] At the group level of a sociolinguistic profile, it means that in some contexts, the language variety used will not be strictly identifiable as "French" or "MA" or "SA," but will in fact comprise an intricate (and rule-governed; again, see Abbasi (1977) and Heath (1983)) mixture of several "varieties." The type of "Arabic" used may vary across a range of registers, perhaps including code-switched/register-switched/borrowed vocabulary or morphology from SA, French or Berber,[10] and even a speaker fluent in all of these languages could conceivably not be a fully competent participant if s/he did not know which to speak when, and how to mix them.

Examples of code-switching and -mixing are common, and not limited to the oral mode: A national brand of fruit preserves is labelled (laḍi:ḍ), in Arabic script, a non-standard spelling that reflects MA pronunciation of the SA (ladi:d), "delicious"; at the same grocery store, the label on the butcher's scale reads, in Latin script, BIZERBA, a transliteration of MA "quickly." Telegrams may only be written in Latin (French) script, but examples of transliterated MA messages have been observed. Conversely, SA orthography may be borrowed for writing MA or Berber, most commonly for personal notes and letters. In Waterbury's *North for the Trade*, for example, the merchant Hadj Brahim recalls: "I used to write my mother and father in *tashelhit* using the Arabic script I had learned at Koran (sic) school" (Waterbury, 1972: 53. See also Gravel, 1979: 79). Almost all products come in ostensibly bi- or multi-lingual packages, but the information provided in each language is often not identical; to have access to all the packaging information, then; a consumer must read more than one language.[11] In other cases, written information is more strictly bilingual. On postal money-order forms and the destination signs at a large city busstop, for example, a reading knowledge of either SA or French is sufficient. Television news, where official visits between heads of state and other international and national political topics are the usual fare, is in a Moroccan-accented SA. The weather, however—of immediate daily concern to a population still more than half rural/agricultural—is in MA. So are most advertisements. The king, during a nationally broadcast speech commemorating the Green March,[12] began in a formal SA, later switched into MA for emotional immediacy ("I've lived among you, shared your bread"), and ended with a flourish of SA, the voice of political and religious authority.

While various kinds of code-switching and -mixing are widespread, they are generally deplored (when not entirely unacknowledged) by those who use them. Of the respondants to Bentahila's language attitudes questionnaire, 75% "expressed their disapproval of code-switching, their attitudes ranging from pity to disgust" (Bentahila 1983: 37). Only 9.17% of his participants called it "an acceptable strategy of communication" (1983: 38).[13] For speakers, and for the scholars who study them, the mixing up of ideally discrete "varieties" goes against the classificatory grain. It is hard to construct a chart or a table when the lines between categories cannot be neatly drawn. Yet if the accuracy of a sociolinguistic profile is to affect the success of any language policy that works from it,[14] a realistic profile of language use and distribution in Morocco must loosen the lines between idealized "languages" and take code-switching and -mixing into account.

Language Policy Since 1956

On the eve of independence from France in 1956, almost every civil servant working in the Ministry of Education was French, as were over half of all teachers (this figure being much higher at the secondary and post-secondary levels, where the vast majority of teachers were not Moroccan nationals). Only about 12% of the school-aged population (aged 7–14), for these statistics (Gallagher, 1958) was enrolled in school, as "French policy was to educate a small, controllable native Moroccan elite rather than to provide mass European education" (Heath, 1983: 18). In his 1956 Speech from the Throne, King Mohamed V first spoke of the "Arabization" of education, a process involving four interrelated sets of problems, known as "unification," "moroccanization," "generalization," and the "modernization/standardization" of the Arabic language itself.

At the time of Moroccan independence there were three separate types of education in Morocco, each having grown out of a different set of historical (and, concurrently, linguistic) circumstances. The Arabo-Islamic system, dating back to the earliest Arab conquests of the seventh century, included (1) Qur'anic schools, which offered introductory reading and writing instruction, but centered on memorizing the Qur'an, (2) medrasas and zaouias, where Arabic grammar and literature as well as beginning level Islamic theology and jurisprudence were taught, and (3) Islamic universities, the oldest and most prestigious of which was the famed Karaouiyine University in Fes, founded in 859 (see Wagner and Lotfi, 1980). Under the Protectorate, the French introduced a system of secular public schools based on their own system. Aside from the few hours a week devoted to Arabic language and Islamic Civilization (the number of hours varied from school to school) all subjects were taught in French. In the "franco-berber" schools, instruction in Arabic was all but eliminated, in the divide-and-rule effort to split "Berbers" from "Arabs." Enrollment in all of these schools, whose "goal was essentially to train subaltern personnel for the administrative and technical services of the Protectorate" (Moatassime, 1978: 30 my translation), was limited to a tiny elite. The *écoles libres*, the third type, were created by Moroccan nationalists content with neither of the above systems. After various unsuccessful attempts at renovating the Qur'anic schools, they began to found the *écoles libres* in the 1930s, private schools modelled after the French system, but using Arabic as the language of instruction (Moatassime, 1978). The goal of this unification was to make some order of these disparate and internally heterogeneous systems, and to this end the public *école nationale* was established.

"Moroccanization" of personnel and "generalization" of instruction to a wider population combined to pose formidable problems which continue to face Morocco even today, thirty years later, as foreign teachers are phased out and the number of students increases annually. The first academic year following independence saw the entry of 150,000 new pupils into the school system, compared to the usual 25,000 or so of Protectorate years, at the same time as 2000 French teachers were lost. The combined effects of this loss of teachers and massive influx of students caused enormous problems of overcrowding that year, "with as many as 110 children in some classes" (Gallagher, 1958: 5). School attendance was made compulsory for children aged 7–13 by a royal degree *(dahir)* in 1963. Half of Morocco's population is under the age of 20, with a growth rate of 3%—among the world's highest. Between 1971–81, as a result of these combined factors, school enrollment more than doubled.

Finally, the "modernization" and "standardization" of the Arabic language is a process which concerns all of the Arabic-speaking and -writing world.[15] In a comparative study of Classical and Iraqi Arabic, Altoma (1970 (1974)) discusses two orthographic problems often cited by advocates of modernizing the Arabic writing system: (1) the "plurality of letter variations" (i.e., the different shapes of each letter in word-initial, -medial, and -final positions) which are said to cause both economic and educational difficulties (too costly to print, and too numerous to learn readily), and (2) the absence of short vowel markings, which "makes it difficult to read correctly without a large measure of alertness and discrimination, even for well-educated readers"[16] (1970 (1974): 283). Altoma also outlines proposed "reforms" of Classical Arabic (SA) grammar, and the creation of a standardized scientific and technical vocabulary.

To facilitate the modernization/standardization process, in 1960 the Institute of Studies and Research for Arabization was founded, as part of Mohammed V University in Rabat. The Institute's first goals were to compile a picture dictionary for use in the primary grades and a French-Arabic dictionary of administrative terminology, "then to turn to a general expansion of Arabic in the fields of science, and finally to develop the linguistic base for the Arabization of the three cycles of education over 15 to 20 years"

(Zartman, 1964: 190). Since its inception, the Institute has concentrated on the development and standardization of Arabic as a modern language of science and technology. Its lexicographers have produced dictionaries of general administrative terms, technical equipment, math, physics and natural sciences, banking, and finance. In an effort to remedy the orthographic problems mentioned above, the "Unified Arabic Code" was developed which, by reducing the number of letter-variants (by breaking letters into their component parts) and (re-) introducing partial vowelling, has made the Arabic alphabet more efficient for typing, more economical for typesetting and printing, and in the process, adapted for use in computers.

In fact, much of the Institute's current work seems to focus on making Arabic computerizable and at the same time intertranslatable with Western technical languages, primarily French and English. One heavily-financed project, for example, is the compilation of a computerized quadri-lingual (Arabic, Latin, French, and English) technical dictionary. This high-tech approach to modernizing the Arabic language is an ambitious undertaking, but whether it is possible to make Arabic into a generative technical language—that is, whether all these newly-minted, -computerized terms will come to be widely accepted and used—remains to be seen. For now, scientific and technical fields continue to operate in French and, increasingly, in English. High school science classes are still taught in French, although Arabization is working its way up through the educational system (see below), and the Institute's linguistic products may yet find a ready market.

These sets of problems have been juggled by policy-makers from 1956 onwards in their attempts to formulate a program of Arabization. The fortunes of these successive programs, though, have risen and fallen along with the political fortunes of their proponents, so that the implementation of a given program was often barely off the ground before a new one was proclaimed in its place, without sufficient time for evaluation or continuity.[17] And even as Arabization was being loudly championed and hastily legislated, as Moroccan nationals replaced the French personnel in government bureaucracies and clerical jobs, there was an increasing demand for persons with a knowledge of French. As Heath (1983) explains:

> To satisfy this need, it was necessary to greatly expand the teaching of French in schools, and for this purpose a large number of French nationals were imported or kept on as teachers, not only of the French language itself, but also of arithmetic, science, and other academic subjects . . . In this fashion, French achieved far greater currency in postcolonial Morocco than it had in the colonial period itself, even though the native French population declined. Most Moroccan intellectuals in this period were educated in France, the French language gradually lost some of its stigma as a language of colonial oppression and became an avenue for socioeconomic advancement. (Heath, 1983: 19–20)

But despite this post-Protectorate expansion of French, and the variability of official language policy, Arabization has made slow progress over the last thirty years. In 1962, the Ministry of Justice was declared Arabized, as were the Faculty of Law's juridical studies[18] in 1975. A 1977 *dahir* (royal decree) proclaimed that all correspondence between citizens and the government, and between "non-technical" government departments would be in Arabic, and "important government documents" would be translated into Arabic. By the 1984–85 academic year, the *ecole nationale* had been Arabized up through the second year of (first cycle) secondary school-that is, all subjects were taught in Arabic, except for French itself which is taught as a foreign language. The third year of secondary school was scheduled to be Arabized the following year.

The Arabization of Education—Policy vs. Practice

On paper, the statement that classroom instruction has been "Arabized" up through the second and third year of secondary school seems straightforward enough. But what does such a policy mean in classroom practice, to the teachers and students it most directly affects? What looks to be a smooth transition from one policy to another when a given subject is Arabized—this year math will be studied in French, next year in Standard Arabic—is in reality a complicated undertaking which places differing demands on its different participants according to their previous training and abilities.

As an example, let us take the case of Youssef, a first cycle (junior high) math instructor in a Marrakech secondary school.

After studying for five years in a private French school (a prestigious Protectorate holdover) whose curriculum included only one and a half hours per week of Arabic language study, his certificate of primary studies exam was given entirely in French. He transferred at that time to a public secondary school, but because he pursued a math and sciences program, he studied Arabic language and literature, and the accompanying Islamic Civilization, for only four to six hours per week during his seven years of secondary schooling. At the regional teacher-training college following graduation, he chose to specialize in math, where all courses were taught in French, save a nominal two hours per week of Arabic grammar. Since finishing his studies in 1978, he has taught all four levels of first cycle secondary school math.

From 1978–84, these courses were taught in French, using French textbooks, French pedagogy, and the French language for all instruction and explanation (and even, claims Youssef, for disciplining students and making extra-curricular announcements).[19] In the fall of 1984, however, Arabization finally worked its way up into his classroom. His two classes of fourth-year math were to be taught in French as always, but for an hour a day, he was expected to teach math to a class of second-year students in Standard Arabic, never having studied it himself in that language.

He did not enter the classroom that fall wholly unprepared. The previous spring and summer he had attended two ten-day Arabization ("re-") training sessions sponsored by the Ministry of Education. At these sessions participants translated French textbooks into Arabic, attended lectures, and took part in discussions and practice lessons where they could exchange observations, corrections, and suggestions. Trainees were also provided with a French-Arabic math lexicon to aid in future translation problems.[20] Thus armed, they were sent off to teach in their now-Arabized classrooms.

Youssef's confidence in the efficacy of these re-training periods seemed to waver. At one point in our discussion, he admitted that the two sessions were not enough, that they (the teachers) could use another, more comprehensive session focused more generally on the Arabic language, not just on terminology translation; later, however, he said that given the new review book (see footnote 20), and another few years of practice, his level of SA would be comfortably adequate for doing his job. For that first class of second-year students (1984–85), he felt unprepared at first, spent much more time than usual planning his lessons, and felt ill at ease in class, but by the end of that year, he estimated that about 80% of his classroom talk was in SA. There are numerous reasons, political and personal, for making such an optimistic assertion, but failing the observational data to substantiate it,[21] Youssef's claim should at least be tempered by a contrasting case.

To find out more about patterns of language use in recently Arabized math classes, observations[22] were made in a Middle Atlas village school in the spring of 1985. The first-grade teacher of the class observed spoke a mixture of SA and MA,[23] at the far MA-end of the MA-SA continuum for commands like "look at the chalkboard" and "show me your slates," and becoming more standardized for actually working the problems, though he never spoke, during the observations, a full sentence that could be classed as wholly "Standard." When the students went to the chalkboard to write an exercise, they narrated their work in a kind of Standard-flavored MA, saying [sitta] (MA [stta]) and [tis'a] (MA [tsa'ud]), [fi] (MA [f]) and [bi] (MA [b]), but otherwise speaking an Arabic much more Moroccan than Standard. Nor was the written language used in this class free from non-SA "impurities." Numbers, as in the rest of formerly-French North Africa, were written Western-style (not the actual Arabic numbers used in the Middle East) and quantity terms (e.g., centimeter, kilogram, meter) are abbreviated in Latin (French) script (cm., k., m.). In addition, though the Arabic text was written from right to left, equations and the like went from left to right, sometimes creating spacing difficulties when the area required for working a given problem was underestimated, and the equation ran into the text.

After the lesson, the teacher explained to me that he purposely uses MA in his class, "so the students' math problems won't be compounded by language problems." There are other possible explanations as well. In the two-teachers-per-class system at the fifth grade level, the Arabic teacher also teaches history and geography while the math teacher doubles as French instructor. Educated under some variety of the old, not yet Arabized system, it is probably no accident that a teacher with far more training in French than in SA would find MA—his own language—the best medium of instruction when French was no longer an option.[24] Perhaps Youssef was fortunate enough to pick up enough SA along the way to be musterable for use later on, with some additional practice and training. How many teachers were not? It seems doubtful, despite Youssef's optimistic assertions to the contrary, that one or two ten-day brush-up sessions, a bilingual subject lexicon, and a home-review book, will be enough to prepare French-trained instructors to teach in SA. How often does "Arabization" mean converting the language of (oral) classroom activity to MA, or some intermediate variety, whether by choice, by default, or some combination of the two? And if the SA called for in official policy is at best only unevenly used in the classroom, how are students to hear or practice enough of it to develop fluency?[25]

Many teachers, then, find themselves caught between the transitional cracks of these changing systems. On the other side of the desk are a large percentage of students caught between cracks of their own. Moroccan students, in a system modelled after the French, take a series of exams at the end of each school year. If a student's composite average falls below the passing minimum, s/he must retake ("redouble") the entire year over again. Each year, 30, 40, 50% or more of a given class may have to retake the following year; it is a rare student who does not redouble at least once in the course of her/his schooling. This system of setbacks and false starts, when combined with a language policy that progressively "Arabizes" one grade level per year, creates potentially serious problems of not-yet-"Arabized" students who redouble themselves back into a now "Arabized" class. A third-year secondary student who has studied math only in French for seven or eight years, might suddenly find him/herself expected to carry on her/his studies in Arabic, with a classful of fellows who have been doing so all along.[26,27]

Different schools have different procedures for accommodating such students. In some, they are placed in special French sections and allowed to continue as before. In others, they are put in special, remedial Arabic sections, which move at a slower pace than the regular ones. Other such students are simply assigned to a regular Arabized section and left to fend. All of these procedures have their drawbacks, either postponing a student's eventual adaptation to a soon-to-be-Arabized workplace or university,[28] or retarding a student's progress in a given subject, or, at worst, dooming a student to failure in a sink-or-swim situation that makes no allowances for her/his linguistic unpreparedness. Conversely, those "Arabized" students who reach the university may find that pharmacy, medicine, engineering, economics, and so on, are still studied in French. If so, a session of "terminology translation" and a complimentary technical dictionary may not be enough to fit them for studying these subjects in a foreign language. The not-so-smooth transition from one educational language policy to another might involve over 50% of the students enrolled over a 15–20 year period (see Moatassime, 1974). The confusion it causes might well leave these students, as is often claimed by their teachers, and by older former students of previous systems, unprepared to "function" in either SA or French and less well-trained in the subjects that are taught in them, in effect producing an enormous ill-educated "lost generation" of sorts (see Bentahila, 1983: 125–126).

Conclusion

Part of the problem is of course a result of political/economic factors. Indeed, the argument has often been advanced that an "Arabization" which advertises itself as a way to equalize opportunity may in reality act to perpetuate the pre-independence elitism institutionalized in exclusive private schools that continue to emphasize French.[29] But part of it is, in a sense, a problem of classification. Like the sociolinguistic profile that could not (realistically) be squeezed into tidy rows and columns, Morocco's current policy of Arabization has not followed the smooth path of implementation idealized by its planners. What on paper appears to be a swift and orderly shift from one policy of language use to another, is in practice a slower and messier business.

If indeed the goal of Morocco's current language policy is the eventual Arabization of the nation's administration, education, and economy (a necessary, if unverifiable, assumption, if one is to work at effecting the stated policy), the changeover will require more than the 10–20 years projected for Arabizing the schools. Provisions must be made for a long period of transitional bilingualism (the actual state of things, though not the official one) until the last of those trained under the old system(s) have finally been replaced by a younger, differently trained generation. A developing nation cannot afford to waste trained personnel in an over-hasty switch from one policy to another. By allowing the already educated to make full use of their training, rather than spending limited resources on inadequate retraining efforts, a prudent policy would steer a compromise between symbolic/linguistic and economic/productive goals.

Just as sociolinguistic profiles end up looking somehow neater than the real-world patterns of language use on which they are based, so planning models *for* language use tend to project fewer complexities than actually occur in the course of their implementation. If sociolinguistic models are to be useful descriptive tools, they must be built up from analyses of language use in social contexts, and forego Cartesian lines of classification if the data do not yield them up.

Every "descriptive" statement about language is also necessarily theoretical. Some levels of idealization are nevertheless more useful than others, for specific purposes. It may be useful, for example, to retain the concept of "language variety" for the purpose of discussing language use in schools, but in the case of Morocco, it seems equally useful for a model to allow for switched and/or mixed "varieties." Similarly, if language planning models are to be effectively implemented, they must begin with a realistic assessment of the situation to be planned for, and of the time required to effect any real changes.

Acknowledgement

*Some of the research for this paper was undertaken while the author worked on the Morocco Literacy Project under the auspices of the University of Pennsylvania and the Université Mohamed V. Funding for the project was provided primarily by a grant from the

National Institutes of Health (*14898) to Dr. D. A. Wagner of the University of Pennsylvania.

The author gratefully acknowledges the help of several Moroccan and American colleagues in stimulating and clarifying some of the ideas of this paper. Special thanks to Mohammed Mellouk for providing invaluable reference materials, and to Susan Philips, Daniel Wagner, Mohammed Dahbi, Jennie Spratt, and Jane Hill for their helpful criticism on earlier drafts of this paper.

Notes

1. See Gravel (1979) or Abbasi (1977) for discussions of the regional distribution of these dialects.

2. A much broader range of spoken contexts than SA: "Outside of the schools and certain Arabized *Facultés* within Mohammed V University. CA (SA) is not used in speech . . . CA is never spoken at home or in the streets" (Abbasi, 1977: 192).

3. See also Ferguson (1959b) and Hamzaoui, S. (1976).

4. Witness the growing number of cafes and boutiques sporting names like "Colorado," "Dallas," "Yum Yum Burgers," "Plum Pudding," and "Pretty."

5. Abbasi estimates that among the Berber speakers, "about 45% are monolingual, the rest are bilingual or trilingual" (1977:228).

6. See Hudson (1980: Chapter 2) for a much different model of "language varieties."

7. See Boukous (1979a) for a sociolinguistic profile with similarly neat lines of classification.

8. See Abbasi (1977) and Bentahila (1983) for excellent examples of both inter- and intra-sentential code-switching, and especially Abbasi for description and discussion of the mixed variety he terms "Franco-Arabic."

9. See Hymes (1974) "Toward ethnographies of communication" for discussion of such factors.

10. Little, if any, work has to date been done on Berber-Arabic code-switching and -mixing among bilinguals.

11. This applies only to the minority of Moroccans who can read in any script. See Direction de la statistique, 1984.

12. November 6 (1975), when thousands of Moroccan citizens marched south into the Sahara.

13. Which Bentahila finds "ironic . . . in view of the fact that this speech pattern is a distinctive characteristic of Moroccans" (1983: 37).

14. By no means a proven assumption, but a useful one if theory is to relate to practice.

15. There is as yet no empirical evidence to confirm these assertions.

16. Contrary to frequent assertions that Arabization means *restoring* Arabic to its pre-Protectorate position, Arabic in the 1950s (and 1980s) was and is being

asked to fulfill functions that did not exist in pre-Protectorate times. See Grand-guillaume (1977: 99).

17. For detailed discussions of these changing policies, see Gallagher (1958a and 1958b), Zartman (1964), and Moatassime (1978).

18. Though see Abou-Abdou (1984) on the difficulty of translating legal texts. The original French texts continue to be used "á toutes les étapes des procedures judiciares" (1984: 26).

19. These claims and similar ones later made about SA, offered in the course of an extended informal interview, unfortunately could not be investigated in classroom observations, but are nevertheless useful indicators of Youssef's perceptions of his own language use in the classroom, before and after "Arabization."

20. In March 1985, the Ministry of Education distributed a second book—on Arabic grammar and vocabulary "review"—and instructed the teachers to study it over the summer as preparation for teaching the following fall.

21. School was already out of session by the time of the interview.

22. Brief, and offered here only as a contrast to the suspiciously problem-free scenario above. A fuller study of the complex patterns of oral and written language use in Moroccan primary school math classes is now in progress.

23. Zartman (1964) speaks of the language of primary school instruction twenty years previously as "a hodgepodge of dialectal Moroccan and Classical Arabic, depending on the teacher" (1964: 167).

24. Not all the students benefit equally from this use of MA to supplement SA explanation; though fast becoming fluent in MA, perhaps 60-70% of the students in this classroom were native Berber-speakers. In schools where virtually all students ar Berber-speakers, local Berber teachers may use Berber for the same purpose (Alison Geist, personal communication).

25. See Altoma (1970 (1974)) for a similar argument about Iraqi Arabic.

26. That is, whose textbooks have been in SA, and whose oral work has fallen within some range of the MA to SA spectrum.

27. See Bentahila for discussion of the opposite problem, at an earlier phase of Arabization, when students "began elementary science and arithmetic in Arabic (and) later had to change their routine and suddenly adapt to studying these subjects in French at the end of their primary education" (1983: 125).

28. Should policy changes indeed be implemented as planned.

29. Bentahila (1983) writes of Arabization planners themselves "who never-theless send their own children to French schools, while still preaching Arabiza-tion as best for the masses . . . While such people may publicly express support for the teaching of traditional culture in schools, they are at the same time reluctant to abandon the advantages of a knowledge of the French language and culture for their own children" (1983: 124). And Abbasi (1977) concludes that "(p)roficiency in French, and in the fields that are exclusively taught in it, is indeed the key to penetration of modern life with its desirable advantages, e.g., better jobs, higher standards of living, etc." (1977: 226). See also Grandguillaume (1977: 106) and Moatassime (1974: 626) for a similar argument.

References

Abbasi, A. 1977. A sociolinguistic analysis of multilingualism in Morocco. Unpublished Ph.d. dissertation. University of Texas at Austin. (University Microfilms no. 77-22908).

Abou-Abdou, M. 1984. L'arabisation et ses problèmes. Rabat: EIRA.

Altoma, S. 1970. Language education in Arab countries and the role of the academies. *Reprinted* in Fishman, ed. Advances in Language Planning. The Hague: Mouton, 1974. 279-315.

Bentahila, A. 1979a. Le profil sociolinguistique du Maroc. BESM, No. 40.

1979b. La situation linguistique au Maroc. Europe. No. 602–603.

Direction de la statistique. 1984. Caractéristiques socio-eonomique de la population, d'après le recensement général. Rabat.

Ferguson, C. 1959a. Diglossia. Word 15:325–340.

1959b. Myths about Arabic. *In:* Georgetown Monographs on Languages and Linguistics, 12. Washington D.C.: Georgetown University Press. 75–83.

Gallagher, C. 1958a. The moroccanization of Morocco. *In:* American Universities Field Studies Reports, North Africa Series, Vol. X, No. 5.

1958b. Morocco goes back to school. *In:* AUFS.

1964. Language and Identity. *In:* AUFS.

Grandguillaume, G. 1977. Pour une anthropologie de l'arabisation au Maghreb. Peuples Mediterraneens. No. 1. October-December, 1977.

Gravel, L. 1979. A sociolinguistic investigation of multilingualism in Morocco. Ann Arbor: University Microfilms International.

Hamzaoui, R. 1965. L'académie arabe de Damas et le problème de la modernisation de la langue arabe. Leiden: E. J. Brill.

Hamzaoui, S. 1976. L'arabisation, problème idéologique. RTSS No. 44. 173–211.

Haugen, E. 1972. The Ecology of Language. Stanford, CA: Stanford University Press, 1972. 148–59.

1983. The implementation of corpus planning: theory and practice. *In:* Cobarrubias, J. and Fishman, J., eds., Progress in Language Planning. Berlin, N.Y., Amsterdam: Mouton, 1983.

Heath, J. 1983. From Code-Switching to Borrowing. London: Routledge and Kegan Paul. Chapter 2, Sociolinguistics of Morocco.

Hudson, R.A. 1980. Sociolinguistics. Cambridge: Cambridge University Press.

Hymes, D. 1971. Competence and performance in linguistic theory. *In:* The Acquisition of Language: Models and Methods, eds. Huxley, R., and Ingram, E. London: Tavistock. 3–28.

1974. Foundations in Sociolinguistics. Philadelphia: University of Pennsylvania Press.

Ministry of National Education. 1983. A general Overview of the Institute of Studies and Research for Arabization. Rabat.

Ministere du plan de la formation des cadres. 1982. Population légale du Maroc, d'après le recensement général de la population et de l'habitat. Rabat. May, 1984.

Moatassime, A. 1974. Le bilinguisme sauvage: blocage linguistique, sous-developpment et coopération hypothequée. Revue Tiers Monde. Tome XI. No. 59–60.

1978. La politique de l'enseignement au Maroc de 1957–1977. Maghreb-Machrek. No. 79 29–46.

Nelson, H. 1978. Morocco: A Country Study. Washington, D.C.: American University.

Seckinger, B. 1984. Language planning, theory and practice: The case of Morocco, 1956–present. MS.

UNESCO. N.D.. Government Document 4110–S7.1 Report on Education.

Wagner, D. and Lotfi, A. 1980. Traditional Islamic education in Morocco: Sociohistorical and psychological perspectives. Comparative Education Review. No. 24, 238–251.

Wagner, D., Messick, B., and Spratt, J. 1986. Studying Literacy in Morocco. *In:*. Gilmore, P. and Schieffelin, B. eds., The Acquisition of literacy: Ethnographic perspectives. New York: Ablex.

Waterbury, J. 1972. North for the Trade: The Life and Times of a Berber Merchant. Berkeley, Los Angeles, London: University of California Press.

Zartman, J.W. 1964. Morocco: problems of New Power. N.Y.: Atherton Press. esp. Chapter 5, Social Problems: Arabization of Primary and Secondary Education, 155–95.

Modern Hebrew as a National Language

Robert L. Cooper

Modern Hebrew is an example par excellence of a national language: an indigenous language which its speakers view as uniquely related to their common history, values, and destiny. The use of Hebrew as an everyday language in the land of its birth has helped Israeli Jews to justify and legitimize their sovereignty over a land in which two national movements compete. This paper briefly describes the process whereby modern Hebrew emerged as a symbol of national identity.[1]

Although the ravages of the Roman-Judean wars in the first and second centuries of the present era substantially depleted the Jewish population of Palestine, and although there was a large-scale conversion to Christianity by the remaining Jews during the Byzantine period, a remnant of Jewry survived and lived continuously in Palestine until modern times. Their number was augmented by Jews from other communities who returned to Palestine either because they sought asylum from wars or from persecution or because they wanted to study, pray, or be buried in their ancestral land, to which the thrice-daily prayers of their religion refer. Until the nineteenth century, however, immigration was small and sporadic, and reemigration, due to poor economic conditions and to poor conditions of health and personal security, was probably substantial (Bachi, 1977:77).

When local conditions improved somewhat in the mid-nineteenth century, Jewish immigration became continuous, with perhaps 25,000 Jews immigrating between 1850 and 1880. This was a substantial number in comparison with the small size of the total population which around 1890 is thought to have been around 532,000, of whom about 43,000 are estimated to have been Jews (Bachi 1977:32,77).

The developing Jewish population of mid-nineteenth century Palestine was divided into several communities, each speaking its own language. Jews from Eastern Europe spoke Yiddish, Jews from Balkan countries and the Ottoman empire spoke Ladino (Judeo Spanish) and Arabic, and Jews from Africa and Asia spoke Arabic, which was often a Jewish communal variety (Bachi 1977:286). The only language that united them all was Hebrew.

Although Hebrew had been abandoned as a language of everyday communication about 200 C. E., it continued to be used as a written language, not only in prayer and in the study of sacred texts, but also in the composition of legal, scientific, and philosophical texts and secular belles lettres. The number of Hebrew books written between the abandonment of Hebrew as a vernacular and the founding of the state of Israel (1948) is immense, reaching the tens of thousands (Rabin, 1973:9). Until the nineteenth century, a large proportion of the Jewish male population in most countries of the diaspora could read and understand Hebrew, and many could express themselves in writing as well (Rabin 1983:42).

While it is true that between its abandonment and its revival as a vernacular it was used principally as a liturgical and literary language, it was occasionally spoken as a lingua franca by Jews who shared no other language. It appears to have been used by Jews in mid-nineteenth century Palestine as a lingua franca, although in limited contexts such as the market. It is possible, moreover, that in the Ladino- and Arabic-speaking Jewish communities a gradual transition to Hebrew as an all-purpose lingua franca was taking place (Rabin 1973:70). Thus, as Blanc (1968), Fellman (1973, 1974), Rabin (1973) and others have pointed out, the term *revival* is a misnomer. Hebrew is no exception to the rule that once a language has passed out of all use whatsoever, it remains dead. The "revival" of Hebrew refers to its resuscitation as a vernacular, a language of everyday life.

The movement for the revival of Hebrew began in Palestine and in Eastern Europe in the 1880's, under the influence of European national movements, which viewed the language of a people as inseparable from its nationhood. As Rabin (1973:69) has pointed out, however, the Hebrew revival movement differed from many of the language movements associated with European nationalism. Whereas many of the latter attempted to extend the range of a vernacular's functions to include those of literacy, the task of the Hebrew revival movement was to extend the range of a written language to include spoken functions. Whereas the peoples mobilized by European national movements could often be united by a common vernacular, the Jews were divided by their vernaculars. But they could be unified through Hebrew.

A series of pogroms and repressive measures in Russia following the assassination of Czar Alexander II (1881) started a wave of mass emigration of Jews, a small number of whom came to Palestine, then part of the Ottoman empire. Many of those who came to Palestine in those years were young intellectuals, influenced by European ideas of nationalism and imbued with the desire for a life better and different from the one they had known in Russia.

The young idealists who started coming to Palestine in the 1880's welcomed the idea of using Hebrew as an all-purpose vernacular, an idea first promoted by Eliezer Ben Yehuda. He was a young Russian Jew who arrived in Palestine in 1881. An indefatigible promoter of the Hebrew revival, he was the first to speak Hebrew at home and to raise his children in Hebrew.

Between 1881 and 1903, from twenty to thirty thousand Jews arrived (Bachi, 1977:79). They adopted Ben Yehuda's idea of introducing Hebrew as the language of instruction in the schools of the settlements they founded. A system of Hebrew schools was established, including kindergartens (from 1898) and high schools (from 1906). "Between 1900 and 1910 young couples began to enter into matrimony who had gone through the Hebrew school and whose Hebrew speech was fluent and natural. At that time were born the first children in families who spoke nothing but Hebrew in the home, and those babies grew up in Hebrew without anyone making a special effort to assure this. They were the first people, after a lapse of 1,700 years, who knew no language but Hebrew" (Rabin, 1973:73).

Due to conditions caused by the First World War, immigration came virtually to a halt, but it began again under the British, who had captured Palestine from the Ottoman empire in 1918. The British accepted a mandate from the League of Nations in 1922 to administer Palestine and Transjordan, with Palestine defined as the territory west of the Jordan River in the former Turkish districts of Acre, Nablus, and Jerusalem. The Mandatory government declared Hebrew, along with Arabic and English, an official language.

During the period of British rule, the population of Palestine almost tripled, from about 676,000 in 1919 to 1,970,000 in 1947 (Bachi, 1977:40). Both Jews and Muslims, the two major groups, showed the same absolute increase in population, 600,000 each, but in relative terms the increase was much greater for the Jews, who grew eleven times in size, from about 56,000 in 1919 to about 650,000 in 1948 (Bachi, 1977:40). This high rate of increase among the Jews was due mainly to immigration. During this period, most of the immigrants came from Eastern Europe and from Central Europe, initially for political and economic reasons and later due to Nazi persecution. There was also, however, a substantial immigration from the Yemen and other Asian countries during this period.

The establishment of the state of Israel in May 1948 resulted in an enormous wave of immigration, as restrictions on immigration, imposed in 1939, were abolished. Survivors of the Holocaust, unwilling or unable to remain in Europe, were now able to enter Israel. At the same time, a growing sense of insecurity among the Jews of Asia and Africa, combined in some cases with messianic expectations, led to a mass exodus from those continents. During the three and one-half years after the establishment of the state of Israel, close to 700,000 Jews immigrated, more than doubling the Jewish population (Bachi, 1977:79). During the remainder of the 1950's through the end of 1960, almost 300,000 more Jews arrived (Bachi, 1977:79). Altogether, between 1948 through the end of 1978, more than 1,600,000 Jews came to Israel (Goldman, 1980:47), about two and one-half times the number of Jewish inhabitants at the time of independence. In 1950, the proportion of the Jewish population in Israel who had been born abroad was close to 75%. Since then it has been declining. By 1978 it was about 45% (Goldman, 1980:13).

The great waves of immigration which followed the creation of the state swamped the Hebrew speakers in a sea of non-Hebrew languages. But linguistic diversity had long been a feature of the Jewish community in Palestine. Based on data collected during the censuses of 1916–1918, Bachi (1956:197) estimates that if any two Jews met at random during that period the chance that they would share the same principal language was only about one in three.

Even then (Bachi, 1956:194), the most common principal language was Hebrew (40%), followed by Yiddish (36%), Arabic (18%), and Ladino (4%). It is likely that Hebrew was also the chief lingua franca among the Jews of Palestine. This hypothesis is based on the assumption that the language most likely to be shared by interlocutors who did not speak the same mother tongue was Hebrew, if only in its literary form. While the hypothesis is reasonable that Hebrew was the language most likely to be chosen as a lingua franca, it remains a hypothesis which must be checked by the analysis of archival material and by interviews with octogenarians and nonogenarians who can tell us what they remember of those days. This is a task which Ezri Uval, of the Hebrew University, has undertaken.

When the state of Israel was established in 1948, the probability that two speakers drawn at random from the Jewish population would share the same principal language had increased from 32%, at the close of the Ottoman period, to 58% (Bachi, 1956:197). Hebrew was by then the principal language of the bulk of the Jewish population. While the linguistic homogeneity of the Jewish population increased, the linguistic homogeneity of those not using Hebrew decreased (Schmelz and Bachi, 1974:762). That is, the population claiming languages other than Hebrew as principal language became ever more heterogeneous linguistically. The increasing heterogeneity of those not using Hebrew as principal language was due, on the one hand, to the increased variety of languages spoken by immigrants who arrived during the British

Mandate and particularly during the period of mass immigration after the establishment of the state and, on the other, to the marked erosion of Yiddish. Whereas in the censuses of 1916–1918 close to 60% of all Jews who did not speak Hebrew as principal language spoke Yiddish, by 1972 that figure had dropped to 19% for those aged 14 or older (Bachi, 1977:290). Of the eight languages listed by Bachi (1977:290), Yiddish is the only language whose percentage among non-Hebrew speakers has declined in each of the five periods reported from 1916 to 1972, even between 1948 and 1954 when large numbers of Yiddish-speaking immigrants arrived.

Perhaps the precipitous decline of Yiddish has stemmed in part from its decreasing usefulness as a lingua franca. As Greenberg (1965) points out, the more persons who use a lingua franca, the more useful it becomes and the more it exerts pressure on others to learn it too. He also points out that nothing stops the spread of a lingua franca more surely than the existence of a rival lingua franca. If our hypothesis is correct that Hebrew was the chief lingua franca between Jews by the end of the Ottoman period, then its spread created pressure on others to learn it and prevented the spread of its chief rival Yiddish. The potential of Yiddish as lingua franca was probably undermined, in addition, by the fact that where opposition existed to the use of Hebrew for secular purposes, it was found among "old-fashioned" ultra-orthodox persons of Eastern European background. Almost all of these spoke Yiddish and thus had no need of a lingua franca with one another. If the opponents to Hebrew for secular purposes had been linguistically heterogeneous, Yiddish would have been their probable choice of lingua franca because Yiddish was spoken by the greatest number of persons who did not claim Hebrew as principal language. As it was, the opponents to Hebrew were linguistically homogeneous whereas those not opposed to Hebrew were linguistically heterogeneous. So the field was left clear for Hebrew.

The linguistic diversity created by immigration has promoted organized efforts to help newcomers learn Hebrew. These efforts are considerable. The state subsidizes Hebrew courses for new immigrants and a substantial proportion of new immigrants enroll. Among the Rumanian immigrants studied by Hofman and Fisherman (1971), for example, as well as among the immigrants in Rosenbaum's (1983) sample, about 40% had studied Hebrew formally in Israel. In addition, news is broadcast several times a day in simplified Hebrew spoken at a slower rate, and a weekly newspaper is produced in simplified Hebrew.

Whereas organized efforts to promote the status of Hebrew are now confined chiefly to helping immigrants learn the language, organized efforts in the early part of the century were of a different character. There were at least three types of activity. First, there was an effort to modernize the language and to standardize new terms. This is an effort which continues today but which was especially important when the lack of vocabulary for everday items and activities was keenly felt. While we can not be sure, it is reasonable that equipping Hebrew to serve as an all-purpose medium encouraged people to use it. Wherever possible, new terms were derived from existing Hebrew words or roots. Modernization was not purchased at the cost of authenticity.

Second, there were the efforts of teachers to promote Hebrew as a language of instruction, which culminated in the "Language War", which Rabin (1973:75) has called the "first national struggle" of modern Jewish Palestine. A German-Jewish foundation for the advancement of Jews in technologically underdeveloped countries, the Hilfsverein der Deutschen Juden, planned to set up a technical high school in Haifa. The foundation operated a number of schools in Palestine, all of which used Hebrew as the medium of instruction. Nonetheless, the Hilfsverein felt obliged to promote German as a language of culture and its promotion of German in the curriculum of its schools aroused resentment. When the Hilfsverein announced in 1913 that its new "Technikum" was to use not Hebrew but German as the language of instruction, on the grounds that Hebrew was not sufficiently developed for work in the sciences, the resentment exploded. The teachers left the organization's schools and took their pupils with them. The boycott prevented the implementation of the Hilfsverein's decision. In Rabin's words (1973:75): "The Jewish population of Palestine acted on this occasion according to the patterns of national struggle, and we shall hardly go wrong if we consider the Language War episode as the first proof that indeed there had come into being in Palestine a modern Jewish nation, on a predominantly linguistic basis".

The third type of organized effort involved encouraging people to use Hebrew. For example, a youth organization, the Gedud Meginnei Hasafah ("Language Protection Legion"), was founded in 1923 to combat the use of languages other than Hebrew and remained in existence until the late 1930's (Wigoder, 1972:1000). Among its activities was the distribution of posters bearing the legend, *Ivri, daber Ivrit!* ("Hebrew [person], speak Hebrew!").

At least until the victory of Hebrew in the Language War and probably continuing through much of the Mandate period as well, the goals of Hebrew promoters were the goals of the Jewish national movement—the return of the Jewish people to the land of its yearning. Hebrew was a central symbol for the awakening and maintenance of nationalist sentiment. To promote Hebrew was to remind its users of the glorious tradition of which they were the heirs and of the political self-determination which they might win for the Jewish people. Hebrew was not only the vehicle of a classical literary and religious culture but it had also been the medium of the Jews' former political sovereignty. In principle, any common language can serve to mobilize the masses, but an indigenous language, carrier of a great classical, religious, and political tradition, which can be claimed as the heritage of the entire group, is a particularly powerful symbol around which to rally.

Once the ascendancy of Hebrew as the chief Jewish lingua franca in Palestine was assured, there was a change in emphasis in the national goals served by the promotion of Hebrew. A vehicle of mass communication was needed to integrate the diverse ethnic groups which were drawn together, particularly after the mass immigration following the establishment of the state, and to facilitate the administration of national institutions. This is not to say that Hebrew lost its role as a symbol of national identity. Indeed, one could argue that it grew more important as a national symbol the more ethnolinguistically diverse the population became. What is suggested here is that efforts which were at first directed towards exploiting the symbolic value of Hebrew, in order to mobilize the Jews in their struggle for self-determination, were redirected, once the struggle was won, towards strengthening Hebrew's position as a vehicle of mass communication, in order to integrate and control a diverse population. Initial efforts at language planning were directed chiefly towards modernizing Hebrew and encouraging people to use it. Subsequent efforts were directed chiefly towards encouraging people to learn it.

That Hebrew is a symbol of national identity for Israeli Jews is clear. Does Hebrew serve a similar symbolic function in the diaspora? Many diaspora Jews do study Hebrew, mostly within the framework of Jewish schools. Before the establishment of the state of Israel, these schools attempted to teach their pupils those Hebrew-language skills which would equip them to carry out their religious obligations, including the study of sacred texts. After 1948, there has been a growing tendency for the goals of instruction to include fluency in modern spoken Hebrew as well.

What purposes are likely to be served by learning modern Israeli Hebrew in the diaspora? Practical secular purposes are likely to be minimal. Most diaspora Jews have little interest in moving to Israel. Learning modern Israeli Hebrew is not likely to serve as a marker of religious identification either. One can practice orthodox Judaism without knowledge of the Hebrew vernacular. A minority among the most religiously observant, in fact, still believe that the use of Hebrew for secular purposes is a sacrilege. But because modern Hebrew is a preeminent symbol of the Jewish state, knowledge of modern Hebrew can serve as an assertion of identification with Israel, which is viewed positively by most diaspora Jews, religiously observant or not. To the extent that diaspora Jews identify with Israel (and one can identify with Israel without any intention of living there), it is likely that modern Hebrew serves as a symbol of Jewish national identity, not only in Israel but in the diaspora as well.

The foregoing account can be summarized as follows. Hebrew was a unifying factor for millennia before the rise of modern national movements. When the movement for the restoration of Jewish political self-determination arose, Hebrew served as a symbol around which national sentiment could be mobilized. After self-determination was realized, Hebrew became a medium for the integration and control of a diverse population, continuing as a symbol of national identity among the Jews living in their ancestral land and becoming a symbol of Jewish national identity for many Jews in the lands beyond.

Notes

1. Much of the material in this article appears in Cooper (1984).)

References

Bachi, R. 1956. "A Statistical Analysis of the Revival of Hebrew in Israel." *Scripta Hierosolymitana*, 3:179–247.

Bachi, R. 1977. *The Population of Israel*. Jerusalem: The Institute of Contemporary Jewry. The Hebrew University of Jerusalem, in conjuction with the Demographic Center of the Prime Minister's Office in Israel.

Blanc, H. 1968. "The Israeli Koine as an Emergent National Standard." In J. A. Fishman, C. A. Ferguson, and J. Das Gupta eds., *Language Problems of Developing Nations*. New York: Wiley, 237–251.

Cooper, R. L. 1984. A framework for the description of language spread: the case of modern Hebrew. *International Social Science Journal*, 99: 87–112.

Fellman, J. 1973. "Concerning the 'Revival' of the Hebrew Language." *Anthropological Linguistics*, 15: 250–257.

Fellman, J. 1974. *The Revival of a Classical Tongue: Eliezer Ben Yehuda and the Modern Hebrew Language*. The Hague: Mouton.

Goldman, M. ed. 1980. *Society in Israel, 1980: Statistical Highlights*. Jerusalem: Central Bureau of Statistics.

Greenberg, J. H. 1965. Urbanism, migration, and language. In H. Kuper ed., *Urbanization and Migration in West Africa*. Berkeley and Los Angeles: University of California Press, 50–59, 189.

Hofman, J. and H. Fisherman. 1971. "Language Shift and Language Maintenance in Israel." *International Migration Review*, 5: 204–226.

Rabin, Ch. 1973. *A Short History of the Hebrew Language*. Jerusalem: The Jewish Agency.

Rabin, Ch. 1983. "The Sociology of Normativism in Israeli Hebrew." *International Journal of the Sociology of Language*, 41: 41–56.

Rosenbaum, Y. 1983. "Hebrew Adoption among New Immigrants to Israel: the First Three Years." *International Journal of the Sociology of Language*, 41:115–130.

Schmelz, U. O. and R. Bachi. 1974. "Hebrew as Everyday Language of the Jews in Israel—Statistical Appraisal." In American Academy for Jewish Research, *Salo Wittmayer Baron Jubilee Volume: on the Occasion of His Eightieth Birthday*. Volume 2, English section. New York: Columbia University Press, 745–785.

Wigoder, G. 1972. "Israel, State of (Cultural Life)." *Encyclopedia Judaica*. Volume 9. Jerusalem: Keter Publishing House, 996–1020.

The Emergence of the National Language in Ethiopia: An Historical Perspective.

Mulugeta Seyoum

The emergence and development of national languages are generallly coterminous with the growth of nations. It is usually along with and equal to the progress made by their respective societies that vernacular languages become media of literature and develop their grammatical, lexical, orthoepic, and orthographic norms. It is also in response to their society's communication needs that their vocabularies expand and their spread across social and spatial boundaries are effected. Thus, the development of national languages is primarily conditioned by the type and extent of the political, economic, social, and cultural progress achieved in their respective societies and not by the particular nature of their linguistic structures. For the most part "the other major elements of nationality such as political and educational institutions, literature, territory, group loyalities and nationalistic movements, and frequently even sovereign states and customs areas are closely interconnected with the language factor" (Deutch 1968:598).

However, the factors that form the basis for the emergence and growth of national languages are not the same everywhere. They vary in time and space. "The concrete historical circumstances, the period in which the foundations for a national literary language are laid, the degree of dialect persistence, and above all, the character of the language relationship of the national period" (Guxman 1968:778) differ from case to case. Within this general framework, the formation, the growth and the nature of the national language in Ethiopia is examined below.

1. *The Sociocultural Background*

Ethiopia has been aptly described as "un museo di populi" (Conti Rossini 1935). Certainly, Ethiopia is ethnically diverse and culturally plural, and this is not a present day phenomenon only. Heterogeneity has always been one of Ethiopia's distinguishing features. For millenia, speakers of various Cushitic, Nilotic, Omotic, and Semitic languages have cohabited in Ethiopia. Major religions, such as Christianity, Islam, and Judaism, along with traditional religions, have also been practiced by one group or another. All these have acted and reacted upon one another making a fundamental cultural unity of Ethiopia (Levine 1974). Linguistically, both from the languages genetic relationships and from the long and close interactions of these various tongues, Ethiopia has become a distinct linguistic area (Ferguson 1976).

The relationship of the peoples that made Ethiopia has been variable. Sometimes it was close, at other times distant and loose. At times it was peaceful and amicable; at others it was characterized by feuding and fighting. The relationship might have been "now thin and localized, now extensive and profound but never absent" (Levine 1974:40). The group that was once the victor had become the vanquished at a later time and vice versa. The extent of the country had changed on several occasions. What was once the center had become the periphery and the periphery the center. Thus, the ally and adversary, the victorious and vanquished, the dominant and dominated, and the privileged and underprivileged distinctions were to be made at any one time in the long history of the country. It was these kinds of relationships that enabled some groups to impose their will, including their cultures and languages. In the process, the relative statuses and functions of the various languages have been determined. Consequently, some languages have come to be used more widely and for more diversified purposes than others.

2. The Language Situation

The Ethiopian language situation is certainly complex. Some seventy distinct languages, each with its dialects, are spoken within the borders of the country. Of these, only three —Amharic, Oromo, and Tigrigna—are spoken by over a million speakers. According to the latest figures (Bender et al. 1976), the mother-tongue speakers of these three languages account for three-quarters of the entire population. It is believed that each is spoken by 32%, 28% and 14.5%, respectively. These are what Ferguson (1966) would call major languages. The rest of the Ethiopian languages are spoken by 25% of the population. Out of these, about ten have been identified as minor languages. That leaves 80% of the langauges "which are spoken by small numbers of people, often only several thousand or even fewer" (Bender 1976:12).

The uses of most Ethiopian languages are thus very limited. They are of local significance only. Those that have cross-cultural functions are few in number. Among the minor languages, Afar, Somali, Wellayita and Keffa-mocha function as such, but they are usually limited to sub-regional levels. The functions of the major languages are relatively extensive. Tigrigna is the major contact language in the two northern Administrative Regions of Tigray and Eritrea. Oromo is the contact tongue in the Southern, Western, and Eastern Regions. By comparison, both the number of speakers and the size of the area where Oromo is spoken are by far greater than those of Tigrigna, but as a contact language, Oromo is strictly regional also.

The only language of national significance is Amharic. Like Oromo and Tigrigna, it too has its regional base—the central highland regions that lie between the Oromo and Tigrigna-speaking areas. Unlike them, however, Amharic has transcended its traditional boundaries. It is now the most learned and widely used language in the country (Bender et al. 1976). Some fifty percent of the country's population is believed to use it in one capacity or another (Richter, Ms).

Ethiopia also has two languages of special purposes, Geez and Arabic. The former is the medium that Christian Ethiopians have used for the last sixteen centuries. It has a rich literary heritage. Until the turn of this century, it was also the primary medium of writing. Arabic is its counterpart among Muslim Ethiopians. In its pidginized varities, Arabic is also used as a contact language in certain communities.

The linguistic situation is rendered even more complex by the superposition of still other languages in recent times. Of these, English stands out. Since the second world war, it has become the primary foreign tongue in the country. It is the medium of instruction in the secondary schools and institutes of higher learning. It is also the sole means of the country's international relations and of acquiring science and technology. Some specialized agencies (technical-oriented institutions) within the country also use English to run their daily business.

The other foreign languages are French and Italian. Their role in present-day Ethiopia is marginal and is increasingly diminishing. In the early days of the advent of modernization, French was the dominant medium in the country. Since the second world war all that has changed, and French has been relegated to an unimportant function/role in Ethiopia. With the gradual diminishing of Italian influence in the country, Italian has also become a marginal language. Unlike English and French, however, Italian in its pidginized variety had become a contact language in some parts of the country. That too is fast diminishing.

3. *The Emergence of the National Language*

An appraisal of the history of Ethiopia readily reveals distinct stages in the development of its national language. For convenience these stages will be considered in chronological order.

3.1 *The Lisane Nigus period*

In terms of historical space, the Lisane Nigus (King's Tongue) period occupies a long span of time. It covers the Aksumite period (from the cradel of Ethiopian civilization up to the end of the first millenium A.D.), the Zagwé era (from the fall of Aksum to the end of the 13th century) and the greater part of the reign of the "Solomonic" dynasty (from the fall of Zagwé to the middle of the last century). Although the historical period under consideration is very long, there is a remarkable similarity between any two points in time in as far as the designation of the common medium, its functions, and the extent of its use were concerned. The medium so chosen was invariably the language of the Nigus (King), hence the name Lisane Nigus (King's tongue). The functions of the Lisane Nigus and the extent of its use had always been limited throughout this period.

3.1.1 The designation of the Lisane Nigus

According to the available sources—oral traditions and written documents—only two languages seem to have attained the Lisane Nigus status. The fist of these is Geez (Old Ethiopic, Ethiopic), which succeeded in obtaining the status during the first millenium of our time. The second tongue to attain prominence for a considerable period of time is Amharic, and its period covers most of the second millenium up to the present.

Geez is one of the tongues which was used in ancient Ethiopia. The extent of its use is not exactly known. The general understanding is that it was spoken by the Aksumites in what is now northern Ethiopia in the administrative regions of Tigray and Eritrea. It is also believed to have been used as a contact language in the Aksumite empire (Ullendorff 1960). Its rise to prominence was due to its association with the sources of political power and social dominance of the period. With Aksum as their capital and cultural center, Geez-speaking monarchs and/or those who favored it had attained hegemony over the rest of the contending forces for a large portion of the time. That made Geez rise to dominant status as opposed to the tongues of the vanquished.

By the first century A.D., the importance of Aksum had started to grow. It became a prosperous trade center. Trade routes to and from Ethiopia all led to Aksum. The sociocultural development of Aksum was such that it induced the development of a writing system. When one became available, it was the language of the dominant group, Geez, that was reduced to writing. On the many stone inscriptions excavated from various sites, Geez happens to be the only language to be employed for the purpose. With the advent of Christianity in the middle of the 4th century, Geez became the sole medium of religion and literary purposes in general. In time, the use of other media, such as Greek, was abandoned in favor of Geez. As the new religion acquired more and more indigenous character, both sacred and secular books were translated and composed in Geez alone. Thus, the association between Geez and writing in general, and religious writing in particular, was cemented early on.

Towards the end of the first millenium, the power and influence of Aksum began to decline. Consequently, socio-political power shifted southwards, first to Lasta (c. 1150–1270) and eventually to Shewa (1270–1974). Since then, the locus of the political scene has moved to and remained in what generally came to be known as an Amharic-speaking area. The "Solomonic" dynasty that ruled the country has been essentially Amharic-speaking. Thus, the association of Amharic with the institutions of power and prestige, the Bète Mengist (Royal Palace) and the person, Niguse Negest (King of Kings) was naturally established and maintained. Because of this association, Amharic came to be known as the Lisane Nigus.

In the domains of religion and literature, Amharic had been unable to make any significant headway for a long time. Until the turn of this century, the status of Geez in these domains was almost a sanctity. In the eyes of the general public, the relationship of Geez and the religion are still sacred. The clergy which monopolized the reading and writing culture did not see any advantage in changing the old medium to Amharic or any other medium. Thus, Amharic, as the Lisane Nigus, and Geez, as the Lisane Sihuf (language/tongue of writing), have since been in a diglossic relationship. The designations were so clear that each language was synonymous with its respective functions.

3.1.2 Struggle for dominance - Lisane Nigus status

As Lisane Negest, neither Amharic nor Geez were without rivals. At Aksum the reign of government was not solely and exclusively controlled by the Geez-speaking monarchs, although they were the most dominant. Political power had changed hands on several occasions. Other language groups, such as the Agnew, Beja, and Felasha, had succeeded, at some time or another, in assuming political power (Getachew, Ms.). Unfortunately, for various reasons, the roles they played and the contributions they made to the making of Ethiopia have not been duly recognized to this day. If anything, they are considered as wanton destructionists of Ethiopian civilization and state. Their leaders are regarded as unlawful usurpers of the throne. In general, the tradition propagated by both state and church has been mainly to undermine the interests and aspirations of these groups. Thus, as of now, we are unable to determine the tongue(s) each of these groups might have used for official duties when they achieved political hegemony and social dominance.

This is very much true of the Zagwé monarchs who effectively dominated the politics of the country for over a century (c. 1150–1250). They, too, are considered as unlawful usurpers of the throne. In spite of their recent history and monumental achievements, like the great rock-hewn churches, they have not been accorded their rightful place in the history and traditions of the country. As kings, the Zagwé monarchs are often despised by both officialdom and church. What reaches us is so meager that we are unable to exactly identify their official tongue.

In the domain of religion, however, they opted for the use of Geez. For religious purposes, the use of Geez in regions adjacent to Aksum began during the Aksumite period. The Agews' acceptance of Geez as the language of the church must have antedated the Zagwé assumption of political power. Furthermore, their decision to continue to use Geez for religious purposes might have been dictated by political considerations also. During the reign of the Zagwé Kings, the glory of Aksum was too fresh to forget and ignore. The Zagwé, residing between the two contenders to the throne—the Aksumites in the north and the Amhara in the south—seem to have chosen to adopt the religion along with its medium for political expediency.

However, the use of Geez for everyday purposes was unlikely. For one, the Zagwé had moved the center of their government from Aksum to Lasta, the heartland of the Agew people. Secondly, the use of Geez for this purpose in Lasta had not been reported. Besides the Zagwé assumed power only after a long and bitter civil war that almost consumed Aksum. In fact, Geez had reportedly become extinct by the time of the ascendance of the Zagwé. It is only logical to imagine, therefore, that the victors, the Zagwé monarchs in this case, used their own tongue, Agew, in the courts they managed and among the army they commanded much in the same way the Amharic-speaking monarchs did after them. This might have been true of others also.

Amharic, as a Lisane Nigus, had also been challenged at various times by different languages. Chief among these were Adal, Oromo (previously called Galla) and Tigrigna. The first of the challenges came from Adal. Adal was the primary political rival of the "Solomonic" dynasty from the beginning. For centuries, the Adalites were conquered and subjugated by the "Solomonic" Christian monarchs. After a long and arduous struggle, Adal gained the upper hand. Under the leadership of Ahmed Gragn (1527–1542), the Christian monarch was conclusively defeated, and a large part of the country came under Adalite influence. In many instances churches and monasteries were looted and burned, and the people converted to Islam. The early and sweeping victories of Adal came to an abrupt end in 1542. In an engagement, Ahmed was killed and his army disbanded in 1542. For fifteen years Ahmed traversed the length and width of the country without having enough time to institute himself as a legitimate national leader and to establish a tradition to that effect. The chances for Adal to rise to prominence and to become a Lisane Nigus was thus lost.

The other language that came much closer to achieving the Lisane Nigus status, or perhaps had done so for a brief period, was Oromo. Since the second half of the 16th century, the presence of the Oromo was increasingly felt in most parts of the country. Following the successful campaign of Ahmed Gragna, the Christian monarch was greatly weakened and transferred his capital from Shewa to Gondar. The Oromo easily moved into more areas than were formerly controlled by the emperor. By the end of the 17th century, the Oromo had "swamped most parts of Shoa

(Shewa) province, reached Amhara, and extended to the southern and eastern regions of Lasta. They settled all along the outer fringes of the plateau in an immense semicircle, leaving untouched only the northern highlands, the area of the old Aksumite kingdom" (Ullendorff 1960:76). Eventually they reached the gate of the imperial capital, Gondar. Gradually they became a power with which to reckon. Many times even the monarchs at Gondar sought their assistance to keep themselves in power.

By and large, the conditions that transpired in the 17th and 18th centuries would have been favorable for the Oromo to become dominant, if they had taken advantage of them. Taken together, the Oromo constituted the strongest force, perhaps because they were not affected by the civil war that wrecked the country. After the death of Ahmed Gragn, Adal had been reduced to a second-rate power. The "Solomonic" monarchs were also so weak that they were virtually prisoners in their royal palace at Gondar. The Oromo were thus able to move to almost all parts of the country without much difficulty.

In spite of all this, however, they did not attempt to assume royal power. Their apparent inability has been attributed to their social system (Abir 1968, Jones and Monroe 1965, Markakis 1974, Rubenson 1968, Trimingham 1952). At that time they had no centralized authority. They were comprised of a loose confederation of tribes, who, for the most part, were engaged in non-sedantatry life. As pasturalist they got what they needed and moved constantly and freely. They fought against all those who deterred their movements, including their own brethren. They did not seem to go to any particular area with the purpose of conquering and subjugation. Besides, "they were quite as willing to fight for the king of Abyssenia (Ethiopia) as against him" (Jones and Monroe 1965:105). Thus having failed or having been unwilling to assume power, although they had the means, the Oromos were not in a position where they could have raised and promoted their culture and language to a national level.

In time, the Oromo settled in various parts of the country. Those who settled in the north alongside the Amhara became farmers. Eventually "a process of assimilation with the earlier Amharic-speaking population started. A Galla nobility emerged and through military service and intermarriage gained political influence on the level of the whole state" (Rubenson 1976:32). Oromo supremacy reached its peak when a half-Oromo prince, Iyoas, was crowned as Niguse Negest in 1755 at Gondar (Budge 1928). With him the chances for Oromo to become a Lisane Nigus became a reality.

Iyoas was crowned at a very tender age, which made it possible for his Oromo mother to rule the country as regent. For that purpose, she summoned her Oromo brothers to assist her in governing the empire from Gondar, an Amharic-speaking heartland. Her brothers came with a large contingent of Oromo soldiers, their households and retainers. Coupled with the large contingent that came with the Queen mother when she first married Iyoas' father, this drastically changed the composition of Gondar. The Oromos had also come and settled in the adjoining provinces, Yejju and Wello, Damot and the Lake Tana region.

In short, the scene seems to have been comforting to Iyoas since he initiated some bold steps. For one, he entrusted most of the important works of the empire to his maternal uncles. Secondly, he chose and used Oromo as the palace language. As Budge (1928:461) noted, "the only language spoken in the palace was Galla, and to all intents and purposes, the capital, Gondar, had become a Galla town. The Galla were not slow to see the opportunity which presented itself to them, and they intrigued and formed a government of their own with the king as their head." But soon the balance of power changed. Iyoas and his maternal uncles were unable to sustain themselves in power. Iyoas was murdered and most of his followers left Gondar (Budge 1928). With that the prominence of Oromo came to an abrupt end.

Following the death of Iyoas, the most important and powerful leader was Ras Michael Suhul of Tigray. Tigray was one of the most important principalities of the empire where contending forces were to rise. Michael had come to Gondar at the behest of the young emperor, Iyoas. Having come to Gondar at the head of a very large and well equipped army, Michael did not lose time in getting himself appointed Ras, the highest rank next to the Nigus, and regent to the emperor. Perhaps because of the intentions of the emperor just discussed, the association between the two did not last long. They became bitter enemies, and the Ras had the emperor killed (Budge 1928). The Ras, however, did not seek the throne, although he could have done so without much difficulty. Instead he chose to use his power to choose one from the royal house and crowned him. Why he selected this course of action is not our concern here. The fact that he did so, however, had some bearing on the identity of the Lisane Nigus. Although the Ras often used Tigrigna in public and it was a commonly used tongue in Gondar (Bruce 1964), Tigrigna did not become the dominant tongue of the time. By not occupying the imperial throne when he could, Ras Michael seems to have denied Tigrigna the symbolic elevation it needed to become a Lisane Nigus. Thus Amharic was able to continue as a Lisane Nigus simply because however weak the person on the throne was, he was Amharic-speaking, and the symbolic bond between the language and the king was not severed.

To comprehend the change of the Lisane Nigus along with the dynasty, we need to examine the type of government that was operating then. The government of that time was inseparable from the person of the king. The two—government and kingship—were integrated in the person of the monarch. The bureaucratic apparatus was essentially the king's household and trusted followers, which made the administrative center of the state. There was no separate administration unit, an institution by itself and distinct from the king's household. There was no structure linking the center with the peripheries other than the occasional and unsystematic personal contacts between the august and his lieutenants. There was no national treasury either. All taxes collected belonged to the monarch. There was no separation between the property of the king and the national treasury. He owned everything and disposed of it as he saw fit. In short, what we had was a government of a household with the king at its head. As it could be imagined, if and when the king was removed (killed or dethroned), the institutions which he created and headed, the ideals and aspirations he valued most and fought for, and the language he chose to use, invariably came to their demise quickly and soon were replaced by those of the new monarch.

Amharic and Geez became prominent languages because the

monarchs that spoke them had essentially controlled the political and social sources of power for most of the time in their respective periods.

3.2 The functions and spread of Amharic as Lisane Nigus

For most of the last seven hundred years, the monarchs that dominated the politics of Ethiopia were Amharic-speaking. But the spread and development of Amharic have been very modest by comparison. The reason for this seems to lie in the sociocultural fabrics of the country.

3.2.1 Simple communicative needs

First, the structure of the government—the type of contact it was capable of establishing and maintaining between itself and the people and among its various principalities—was characteristically simple. The government was person-oriented and was centered on one man, the king. The interaction that was so desired was limited and was conducted on a man to man basis. There was no institutional and systematic contact/correspondence between the royal court and the various principalities. Whatever communication existed between the king and the regional princes was simple and irregular. The kings then were satisfied with any regional leader who paid his annual tributes and remained loyal to them (Taddesse 1972). The payment of tributes essentially constituted the bulk of the communication between them. Other than that, the regional leaders were themselves kings in their own right. They usually maintained independent local courts and were succeeded by their own relatives. As long as they remained loyal to the king, they did whatever they thought was in their best interest. The kings moved to certain regions only when their authority was challenged and moved out as soon as they established law and order or instituted new leaders of their choice.

Another factor that might have inhibited the development and spread of the Lisane Nigus, Amharic, was the constant change of the seat of government. During the reign of Geez-speaking monarchs, the center of the empire was Aksum. During the time of the Zagwé it moved to Lasta, and during that of the "Solomonic" dynasty, it moved further south to Shewa, and lastly to Gondar.

In fact, between the fall of Lasta in 1270, and the founding of Gondar in 1632, there was no fixed capital as such. At this juncture in Ethiopian history the royal "court actually changed its location at regular intervals" (Taddesse 1972:105). By constantly rotating their seat, the emperors were "able to play the role of protector of their people, and at the same time, to ensure the continued loyalty of the local hereditary rulers and royal appointees over them" (Korteen 1972:22).

However, as much as this suited their purposes, the absence of a permanent capital deprived the country of the formation of the means and ways of establishing and maintaining a permanent link between the center and the various regions. Under such circumstances, the development of a cadre of bureaucrats and professionals and the corresponding institutions and culture was hardly possible. Actually, there was no need for any of these. Consequently, the government of this period remained largely remote for the majority of the people or even unknown to some of them. And so was the language that was associated with such a government.

The kings in traditional Ethiopia could have met their communication needs without a common and elaborate tongue. The simple and infrequent interactions between the center and various regions, between the king and his lieutenants, and between the king and the people at large, could have been performed by any tongue. Besides, the regional leaders, who themselves were contenders to the imperial throne, could hardly be expected to use the king's tongue in their semi-independent courts. In fact, their allegiance to the emperor was usually temporary. It was a bid for time. They submitted to the king's authority only as long as he had sufficient power to exercise it. If and when the conditions permitted, these princes declared their sovereignty and/or their contention to the throne. Thus, they could not have been willing agents for the steady use and spread of Amharic, one of the attributes of the king they would have liked to replace. This, however, is not to rule out the exceptions—those regional leaders who saw their fortunes rising in their close association with the king.

The king's contact with the general population was even worse. It was usually short, intermittent and most importantly, it was antagonistic. Following a campaign to subdue a rebellious leader, it was the people that usually received the brunt of the king's wrath. Oftentimes their settlements were burnt and their property looted or destroyed. Sometimes, they were either killed or enslaved. Under such circumstances, it is improbable to imagine a steady growth of the king's influence among his subjects. The Lisane Nigus identified with the king and his wreckless campaign could have hardly won acceptance among the populace.

The other factor that contributed to the stagnation of the Lisane Nigus lies in the nature of the economy which was essentially subsistent. Each community, for that matter, each household was self-sufficint. It produced its own food, clothing and other necessitites. There was no need to go out of one's own community for want of the necessities of life, except salt. The absence of large and permanent towns had also inhibited the growth of internal trade. That is, there was no motivation for the people to produce what they were capable of producing. For the most part, trade was limited to bartering and was conducted among adjacent communities. Trade with other societies was even much more limited.

The only kind of trade that flourised to a certain extent dealt with rare and luxury items (gold, ivory, civet, slaves, etc.). The life of the general population was not greatly affected either at the production or consumption levels. Therefore, "the potential impact of trade in introducing new technologies and forcing social interaction through developing commercial interdependence were little felt by the average peasant" (Korten 1972:29). In linguistic terms, what all this means is that conditions required for the development of a lingua-franca did not arise in traditional Ethiopia. Besides, trade as a profession had not been favored by any of the dominant groups, including the Amhara. Those who were permitted to trade were either foreigners (the Greeks and Arabs) or minorities such as Ethiopian Muslims that spoke different languages. In those days, it was the traders that were learning the languages of their customers and not vice versa. Thus, the growth of a trade language in traditional Ethiopia was curtailed by the limited nature of its commerce, and the web of conflicting interests that existed between those who controlled the commerce and those who controlled the controllers of commerce.

3.2.2 Some favorable factors

Again there were some exceptions. There were two factors that somehow promoted the spread of the Lisane Nigus. One of these was the establishment of military garrisons called Hadaris. The Hadaris were built "at different parts of the kingdom . . . to keep the stability of his (king's) kingdom" (Getachew, Ms). As part of their functions, the Hadaris might have served as centers for the growth of new communities with the language and culture of those who controlled the Hadaris as the core. As the royal army was usually composed of various ethnic groups, its common tongue was Amharic. Whenever the royal army or any segment of it moved and settled some place, Amharic seems to be the medium that went along. But the Hadaris could be composed of only one ethnic group over which the king had control. Hadaris seem to have been built by the Tigré, Adaré, Guragé, Argoba, Gofat, and so on. In cases like these, the Hadaris could not have promoted the king's tongue and culture.

The effectiveness of the Hadaris as language and culture traffickers was further affected by their inability to maintain effective communication with the center. Whenever and wherever the authority of the king declined, the Hadaris were effectively cut off from the center. In time, some like the Argoba and Gafat became assimilated in language and/or culture with the dominant people around them. Hadaris established in regions contiguous to the center—Shewa and Damot—were able to maintain their contact with the center under various circumstances. Thus they were constantly replenished with forces that carried the change even further with these Hadaris as the new centers.

During the heyday of the "Solomonic" dynasty (14th-16th centuries), the most consistent traffickers were the Ethiopian Orthodox Chruch missionaries (Getachew, Ms). The national Church which had benefited from the rise of powerful kings, such as Amde Tsion and Zere Yaiqob, carried Amharic along with the gospel. At times, some zealous missionaries seem to have spread both the religion and the language even further than the regions which were under the effective control of the king. By this period, the Church had reached as far south as the present-day Bale, Sidamo, Keffa and Gamu Goffa regions (Levine 1974, Taddesse 1972). Amharic was then serving as a contact language in these regions and was duely recognized as such by Portuguese travellers (Levine 1974). With the defeat of the Christian monarch by Adal and the subsequent mass movement of the Oromo people, both the Church and Amharic lost ground and were eventually replaced in many of these regions.

The sociocultural factors that prevailed in traditional Ethiopia had not only limited the spread of Amharic but also its functional diversity. Although reading and writing skills had long existed in Ethiopia, Ethiopian culture had remained essentially oral until recently.

Reading and writing skills were limited in many respects. For one, the number of people who could read and write had always been very small. The only institution that needed them on a constant basis was the Church. The Church, as the only institution of learning, seems to have been producing what it needed, both in quantity and quality. The needs of the royal and regional courts were limited and were met by the clergy. Besides these two, there was hardly any need for literacy. The life of the average people did not require any reading or writing skills. The life style of the average educated Ethiopian priest was not any different from the peasants around him and did not attract them en masse. People who read and wrote outside the accepted institutions were considered social deviants. In addition, reading and writing were inherited as occupations. All these contributed to the high degree of illiteracy in the country.

Secondly, literary activities, other than those officially sanctioned by the Church and State, were actively discouraged in traditional Ethiopia. Popular literature in its written form did not develop as part of the general culture. The clergy that had the skill, the time and the luxury to do so were not that successful. The only literary activity they were able to cultivate was a kind of poetry called Qiné. But it was usually composed mainly in Geez and was oral. The poetry that so developed did not go beyond the confines of the Church, and it was unable to employ other tongues. The only tongue that occasionally used it was Amharic, because most of the Quiné schools had thrived in Amharic-speaking areas. Poetry composed in the vernaculars and by the common people was not considered worthy until the recent past.

Lastly, the accepted and established medium of writing was Geez. No other tongue was considered appropriate for the purpose. Amharic was not reduced to writing until after it became the Lisane Nigus. The earliest available document dates back to the 14th century. Even then it was of a limited nature. The documents contain songs glorifying victorious emperors of the 14th and 15th centuries. As these songs were spontaneously produced, the old literary tongue, which was then extinct, could not have been used for the purpose. Thus the choice of Amharic was a practical necessity. Unfortunately, this practice was discontinued. Geez as a written medium reigned virtually unchallenged up to the middle of the 19th century.

However, the Lisane Nigus status which Amharic had assumed since 1270 was not without its advantages. As we have seen, it set Amharic apart and made it prestigious. Consequently, when the opportunities to use a living tongue arose, although admittedly limited, it was Amharic that was chosen for the purpose. The popular songs of the 14th and 15th centuries, and the religious controversy between the Portuguese Jesuits and the Ethiopian clergy were cases in point. Amharic's success in becoming the auxiliary medium of Church functions—services and particularly education—was due to its Lisane Nigus status also. When Geez became extinct and the sociocultural center of the country moved away from the old sites, the continued use of Geez in all the affairs of the Church must have become difficult.

At this time, the sociolinguisitc factor favoring the introduction of Amharic had begun to mature. For example, most of the important learning centers, such as Debre Haiq, Debre Libanos, and Debre Gol, that were later to play significant roles in the affairs of both the Church and the State, were established in the heartland of Amharic-speaking people (Taddesse 1972). The people that came to run these institutions, influence the State and spread the

Gospel in the adjoining regions and beyond were either natives or
were educated in the area. Amharic gradually became the common
working tongue of the then emerging elite. Coupled with its
Lisane Nigus status, this seems to have given Amharic the advantage over the other tongues.

Given the established status and functions of Geez, the use of
Amharic as an auxiliary medium of the Church could only have
been achieved very gradually over an extended period of time. But
in time, Amharic became the common medium of instruction of
the Church school system. At the lower levels, Amharic is the sole
medium because neither the teacher nor the pupils know Geez. At
higher levels, in schools of music, poetry and commentary, where
a good knowledge of Geez is required, Amharic is used as a
medium. Discussions as to the quality of the music, poetry or the
content of the religious text are invariably conducted in Amharic.
The Church had thus been using Amharic rather extensively, but
without acknowledgement. Unintentionally, the Church was
promoting Amharic towards a literary medium.

3.3 Amharic as Yemengist Quanqua

The period of Yemengist Quanqua (language of government)
covers the last hundred years or so that elapsed since the rise of
Tewodros to the imperial throne (1855–1868) heralding the beginning of modern Ethiopia, an Ethiopia with decidedly new and
different needs. The advent of modernization and centralization of
political power have changed the communication needs of the
country favoring the establishment of a common, standard
tongue.

At the foundation of this change is the formation of the modern state of Ethiopia. During the early decades of the 19th century,
Ethiopia was suddenly awakened from its centuries-old isolation
and found that it was encircled by several enemies. The Egyptians,
Turks, Italians, and others had come to its doorsteps and were
threatening to invade the country. The threats were so real that the
various regional leaders were forced to make choices between
remaining divided and risking colonization, and uniting the divided country and forming a strong defence to maintain their

collective sovereignty. Having opted for the former, each major regional leader was actively seeking to unite the country under his or her rule. They allied and reallied and fought against each other until at last one of them emerged victorious. The first to succeed in forging the badly needed unity was Tewodros (1855–1868). With his ascendance to the throne, the dawn of modern Ethiopia and the use of a common medium began.

It must be admitted that Tewodros' success was limited. In fact, his importance lies not in what he achieved but in what he envisioned. What he envisioned was a united, modernized and therefore strong Ethiopia capable of defending its own interest (Rubenson 1976). As part of that vision, he seems to have recognized the need of a common medium. He was reportedly keen in promoting such a medium. His choice was Amharic, perhaps because it was the Lisane Nigus and had on occasion appeared in writing. Tewodros did not seem to prefer Geez for the purpose. If anything, he strongly and openly urged its replacement by Amharic. Even in the domain of religion, his preference for Amharic was direct. When he was presented with a Geez scripture, he was quoted as having said, "Why do you bring such books which nobody understands? The translation (Amharic) is much better" (cited in Brown 1976:311). His pragmatic considerations proved correct in time.

At first, however, the clergy, which dominated the reading and writing culture, resisted his innovation. Among other things, for the clergy, Amharic was a profane tongue and could not be used in place of Geez. Despite the resistence of the clergy, the group he needed to achieve his purposes, Tewodros insisted on using Amharic for writing purposes. He let his chronicle be written in Amharic for the first time ever. Against established tradition, he used to read the Bible in Amharic. To the dissatisfaction of the clergy, he encouraged foreign missionaries to translate, publish and distribute the Holy Scriptures in Amharic and teach in it too (Rubenson 1976). In so doing, he seems to have set a new direction for the spread and use of Amharic. In general terms, his attempts were symbolically comparable to what was done in Europe on the eve of the rise of nationalism which necessistated the use of the various vernaculars in place of the old literary tongues and the corresponding veneration of these vernaculars to national status in their respective countries.

It should be noted that Tewodros did not start from scratch. The use of Amharic, although not in regular fashion, had been noted before Tewodros assumed power. Some of the regional leaders (Sabagadis of Tigray, Wube of Simén and Tigray, Sahile Sillasie of Shewa, and Ras Ali II the Regent) had begun to use Amharic for their official correspondence. Foreign missionaries who had then started operating in various parts of the country had also chosen it over other tongues. They taught and preached in it. Of the many thousands of scriptures they distributed in the country, the great majority were in Amharic (Pankhurst 1962). All these were indicative of the changing conditions, but the actual symbolic transformation of Amharic into a written and official tongue of the emerging nation/state remained until the emperor Tewodros chose it and lent it his status and prestige.

Tewodros did not live long to see what became of his preferred common medium. As part of his vision—modernization of the society and centralization of its political apparatus—Amharic seems to have been inherited and promoted by his successors. Since then, Amharic has been inseparable from the state of modernizing Ethiopia.

The emperor who effectively succeeded Tewodros was Yohannes IV (1872–1889). Following tradition one would expect emperor Yohannes to institute his mother-tongue, Tigrigna, as the official medium of his court, but he did not. He continued to use Amharic for that purpose. Yohannes' preference of Amharic to other tongues for official functions could be explained in one of two ways. One, Amharic might have been sufficiently established as a permanent official medium of the state so that Yohannes had to follow suit. Or, two, the political situation was such that Yohannes found it expedient to continue to use Amharic for official functions. Yohannes' Ethiopia was comprised of Tigray, his home base; Bégémidr and Hmhara, the previous center of the empire; Wello and Yejju of Michael; Gojjam and Damot of Tecle Haimanut; and Shewa and its tributaries of Menlik. Thus, most of the principalities of the empire were under Amharic-speaking regional princes. Besieged by the continued aggression of the country's enemies, Yohannes had sought to maintain the country's unity on which the maintenance of its sovereignty depended to a great extent and for which he subsequently gave his life. Thus, if the choice of an official tongue had political ramifications, it was Amharic that had greater dividends. Besides, he himself was known to have mastered an excellent command of Amharic (Zewdie 1975), thereby making the decision easier for him.

Yohannes' decision to use Amharic for official purposes was also significant on the socio-psychological level, because it demonstrated the tolerance needed for the emergence of a common medium. And tolerance is an important and necessary step towards convergence. Such a step is even more profound when an august decides to use one of his subjects' tongues. Thus by choosing to continue to use Amharic for his official duties, Yohannes seems to have confirmed Amharic's new official status as the language of government.

This transformation of Amharic as a medium of government should not be perceived as a consequence of the choice made by this or that monarch, but primarily as a result of the new social conditions that came to play decidedly important roles in modernizing Ethiopia. For any tongue to rise to such a status and function, the support and continued use of the elite is a necessary but not a sufficient condition. In history, every elite is not always fated to make its imprint permanent. If that were the case, Amharic could have attained this stage a long time ago, because as a Lisane Nigus it was certainly the choice of the emperors for a long time. The crucial factor is the development of the appropriate social conditions under which it would be possible for such persons to lend their prestige to the language of their choice such that it became what they intended it to be. Thus, Tewodros and his successors were able to accomplish their purpose because the conditions were ripe for their actions. The decisions of Tewodros and his successors were prompted by the new social conditions which called for a need of a common tongue.

The period following the reign of Yohannes was even more favorable for the transformation of Amharic in the direction it had begun. For one, the monarchs that reigned until 1974 were all Amharic-speaking. In this regard, the roles Menlik (1889–1913) and Haile Sellasie (1930–1974) played are notable. Secondly, and most importantly, the overall social conditions have changed significantly favoring the extensive use of the common tongue, Amharic.

It was also because of these changing conditions that Amharic was able to replace Geez as Lisane Sihuf (language of writing). The clergy that previously opposed the use of Amharic for writing purposes had become, by the turn of the century, an enthusiastic supporter of the idea and part of the process of change. In fact, at the initial stage, it was the clergy that was called upon to do the job. As functionnaries of the new state, as teachers and writers, they used Amharic rather extensively and benefited from the change. Thus the clergy not only came to terms with the new status and functions of Amharic but also became its ardent propagators. The clergy was thus able to effectively bridge the gap between the old (the writing of Geez) and the new (the use of Amharic). The domains where written Amharic came to be used were for the most part new ones: mass media, public education, and the modern state apparatus. These domains facilitated its acceptability. Thus, the functions and even development of Amharic are commensurate with the modernization of the Ethiopian state and society.

3.3.1 Modern government as a vehicle

By and large, the unification of Ethiopia (save Eritrea) was essentially attained during the reign of Menlik (1889–1913). The old regional kings were effectively brought under his effective control. Their hereditary rulers were relegated to loyal subordinates with little or no power to challenge Menlik's authority. Furthermore, Menlik had also managed to institute modern ways of running the affairs of the country by appointing a cabinet comprising seven ministers (Darkwah 1975:26). Denied of their traditional authority—to impose and collect taxes, raise an army, and promulgate laws and engage in negotiations with foreign governments—the regional leaders suffered a great setback (Markakis 1974).

At the same time, the status and prestige of Menlik were bolstered. The victory he achieved over the Italians in 1896 greatly added to his prestige. With the rise of Haile Sellasie to power, the regional kings had been systematically reduced to non-significant positions. Since 1942, and particularly after the 1960 coup, they have been replaced, for the most part, by appointed officers of the central government. All are now the representatives of the emperor in Addis Ababa. As part of their responsibilities, they carry out the directives and protect the interest of the central authorities.

Consequently, the central government today has the need and the means to reach the people throughout the country and has accordingly structured the government. The administrative apparatus/division of the country is such that the chain of command reaches the remotest part of the country thereby further breaking the old political alliances and allegiances while establishing new ones that enhance the status and prestige of the king(s). The corresponding structure and regular conduct of the affairs of the state seem to have enhanced the new image of the state. That is, the people's concept of government has begun to change from the authority and whims of the powerful (king or regional lord) to that of the collective and the relatively institutionalized body called Mengist (government). This new concept, reinforced by various factors, has been steadily spreading to various parts of the country. And the language which has been used and identified with the new state apparatus, Mengist, is called Yemengist Quanqua (language of government).

3.3.2 Urbanization as an agent

Urbanization, as we know it today, is a recent phenomenon. It started sometime at the turn of the century. After the victory over the Italians in 1896, some measure of peace and order was obtained in the country. Trade slowly but steadily began to grow. The new capital, Addis Ababa, founded at the geographical center of the country also became the new trade center. Highways were built connecting it to some of the important trade centers of some regions. With the establishement of the railways connecting Addis Ababa with part of Djibuti, it came to dominate the country's trade to a point where all imports and exports have to pass through the capital.

From the start, the composition of Addis Ababa was multiethnic and multilingual. The first settlers, the soldiers and retainers of the emperor and those of the various regional governors, were drawn from all parts of the country and represented virtually all ethnic groups. Addis Ababa was simply a macrocosm of the entire country in miniature. The communication needs of this highly multilingual town was met by Amharic. And there seems not to have been any incidence to the contrary. Amharic, as the language of the all-powerful emperor, perhaps was accepted as a logical choice. The fact that Addis Ababa was then a newly founded town might have made the use of Amharic easier than the case would have been if it were an old urban center with an established medium.

As Addis Ababa became increasingly cosmopolitan, its composition has accordingly become increasingly less diverse. In 1910, those who could be considered as Amharic first language speakers were less than one in five. In 1952 that figure rose to fifty percent, and in 1967 to three-quarters of the city's population (Bender et al. 1976). Today, for all intents and purposes, Addis Ababa is an Amharic-speaking city. Amhaic has thus grown with the national capital and has assumed its prestige and has consequently been able to take advantage of its institutions and facilites.

The centralization of the political apparatus and the expansion of trade and communication facilities have facilitated urban centers throughout the country. The old garrison built in the last century has become permanent also. As regional, provincial, and district centers, they offer better opportunities than the countryside around them. Thus the centers have created conditions for interethnic contacts of major proportion. The language that serves the need of such multilingual urban centers is also Amharic. In their survey of 188 towns in Ethiopia, Cooper and Horvath (1976:171–8) found that "Amharic was claimed by the largest number of speakers; it was a majority language (76–100%) in the largest number of towns and a minority language (0–25%) in the smallest number of towns." In fact, urbanization in general has become an agent for the spread of Amharic in rural Ethiopia. This process of diffusion seems to have been facilitated by the presence of a large proportion of Amharic mother-tongue speakers in many of the urban centers (Cooper and Horvath 1976).

Industrialization, as an important aspect of modernization has also promoted the spread of Amharic. In the factories he studied, Cooper (1976b) found that "almost the entire work force knew Amharic." But industrialization has not yet developed in Ethiopia, and its full impact on language diffusion is not yet felt in the country. Amharic, however, is the only tongue that is consistently associated with the technology and associated know-how that accompany industrialization. As things stand now, Amharic seems to have the potential of benefiting from industrialization if and when it is instituted in the country on a large scale.

3.3.3 Modern education

Modern education in particular is the other institution that serves as an agent of diffusion for Amharic in Ethiopia. Given its structure and functions, the educational system is the most consistent and systematic instrument for the continued spread and development of Amharic.

The first organized and state-supported modern schools were established at the turn of the century by Menlik II. Cognizant of the resistence of the powerful nobility and clergy to modern education, he himself became the patron of the new school system. He actively encouraged his lieutenants to do likewise in their respective regions and brought teachers from outside. He also sent his grandson and cousins to these schools in order to set an example (Pankhurst 1962) and perhaps to underscore the importance of these schools in the years to come.

In these early schools only two native tongues, Amharic and Geez, were taught along with French, English, Italian and Arabic. The important languages of education and those most popular among students were French and English, respectively. No significance was attached to either Amharic or Geez. The students did not like them, and they were taught by church- educated persons of relatively low social standing. In time the teaching of Geez was terminated, leaving Amharic as the only native tongue to be taught. Amharic's popularity among students and its importance in the system did not change, although the leaders of the time had spoken on the importance of the learning of Amharic and Geez (Pankhurst 1962).

The fact that Amharic continued to be taught is important in and of itself. Firstly, it gained precedence over Geez, the old language of learning. Secondly, it eventually became part of the institution which was designated for the introduction of modern science and technology. Lastly, it came to be associated with the new educated elite that eventually came to occupy an important place in changing Ethiopia.

The impact of these schools prior to the Italian invasion (1936–1941) was very modest. The small number of educated people were to play important roles. Some became teachers, others civil servants, and still others writers. They were all advocates of modernization. In their respective domains, they helped to raise the consciousness of the general populace, and the medium they chose to use was Amharic.

After the War, the importance of these modern schools grew. Haile Sellasie, who had found his allies in educated people early in his political life, was one of the first to recognize the importance of education. Thus a national educational system was established. The emperor himself was his own Minister of Education. The old schools were re-opened and new ones were also built in various parts of the country. Steadily, but admittedly slowly, the educational system soon began to grow.

Since the War, the languages used in the school system have been English and Amharic. English replaced French as the uncontested medium of education. The status of Amharic vis-à-vis English did not change, but compared to the pre-war years, its status has changed for the better. It has now gained a respectable place in the school system. For one, it began to be used as a medium of instruction for the first three grades. Secondly, and most importantly, it is now taught as one of the three compulsory subjects, including English and math, in the secondary schools. Until recently (1976), it was necessary for students to pass Amharic if they were to go to college. Even when the college entrance exams were prepared in London, Amharic was one of the compulsory subjects. Despite the fact that college education was offered in foreign languages, students were required to pass the Amharic exams. In the process, textbooks to teach Amharic were prepared and improved on several occasions. Above all, Amharic became the accepted common tongue of the rising educated elite. In their capacities as modern civil servants, military and police officers, teachers, writers, journalists, and other professional people continued to use and spread it.

Following the promulgation of the Revised Constitution (1955), which formally decreed Amharic as the official language of the empire, the status of Amharic in the school system has been even further enhanced. In 1964, after some years of preparation and pilot studies, Amharic was made the medium of instruction in the elementary schools throughout the country. The significance of this decision is manifold. The status of Amharic is elevated. Its functional adequacy has been facilitated through the prepartaion of textbooks, teachers' manuals and other teaching materials. Teachers' training institutions began to change their curricula to suit the changing conditions.

Furthermore, the spread of Amharic seems to have become assured. Now that Amharic is the medium of instruction, all school children are exposed to it adequately. Since 1964, school children have been required to take a National General Examination at the end of their sixth year. As elementary education does not guarantee success, the pupils' desire to pass this exam is very high. Given their tender age and motivation, it is most likely that they all learn it very well. In the process, Amharic continues to spread in the areas where schools are opened, perhaps ensuring its place among the next generation.

After its success in the elementary schools, the state had evidently intended to extend the use of Amharic in the secondary schools also (Abraham 1970). To that effect, some projects were undertaken with the support of international institutions. In the summer of 1970, this writer was involved in such an effort. Perhaps because of the rapidly changing conditions, no step was taken in this regard. Recently, the desire to revive the issue is evident. Discussions in the concerned institutions as how to best transfer to the Amharic medium in the secondary schools is underway (Richter, Ms). The Ethiopian Languages Academy seems to be responding to this need, perhaps inadvertently, when it sets out to develop the terminology of Amharic so that it is possible to translate any text up to and including the senior secondary school level.

To this effect, support from UNDP has been obtained. Professionals from various fields are actively engaged in the project. As a result, some degree of success seems to have been achieved. However, given the present language policy, it is doubtful whether such a decision can be made. On the other hand, the language problem is mounting. The level of English proficiency is so low even the best of students who join the various colleges have demonstrated difficulty in following their lectures in English. It is possible that practical problems such as these may serve as catalysts for major decisions to be made in the near future.

In higher education, the place of Amharic has always been limited. Until 1974, only college (Freshman) Amharic was taught at that level. It has since been discontinued. In higher education the language of instruction and administration is English. Amharic is used by the University administration or a faculty or a department only when dealing with government institutions. The only department that uses Amharic for instructional purposes is the Department of Ethiopian Languages and Literature. Since the primary purpose of this department is to train Amharic teachers for the secondary schools, Teachers' Training Institutions and other specialized schools, the status of Amharic has been positively enhanced by this limited use also. Many of the graduates of the department seem to have given the teaching of Amharic in the secondary schools some degree of credence.

The missionary schools have also served as agents for the diffusion of Amharic. As long ago as the 17th century, Amharic was the missionaries' choice, perhaps because Geez was extinct and could not have been an effective medium for the conversion of the people which they were trying to achieve. The use of Amharic by the early missionaries was limited because their stay in the country was short lived. However, they seem to have set the trend.

The second wave of missionaries started to come to Ethiopia in the early eighteen hundreds. They, too, chose to use Amharic. In this regard, what the missionaries of this century have done is more significant. Among other things, their numbers, and therefore, their activities have increased. Most importantly, recently they are required by law to operate in the areas that are considered outside the sphere of influence of the Ethiopian

National Church. In other words, they have been limited, for the most part, to work in regions that are inhabitied by non-Amharic-speaking people. There, they have been teaching Amharic and in Amharic too. Considering the significance of their contributions in literacy, health education, home economics, agriculture and religion, it is not difficult to imagine how much they have advanced the diffusion of Amharic. Through their various activities and publications, they have created conditions where Amharic could be spoken, read and written outside the traditional Amharic-speaking areas.

Another branch of education that also functions as an agent of the diffusion of Amharic is the *National Literacy Program*. In the early days, its impact was modest. Its budget was limited and was mostly staffed by volunteers. The materials used in the program were in Amharic and classes were conducted in it also. Among non-Amharic-speaking participants, the learning of Amharic as a second language and the acquisition of literacy was accomplished at the same time.

Since the 1974 Revolution, the literacy campaign program has changed in several aspects. Among other things, due consideration is given to the langauge diversity of the country. Along with Amharic, four other languages—Oromo, Somali, Tigrigna and Wellayita—are used. Nine others are being studied and may be used in the near future. However, the primary medium of the national literacy campaign is still Amharic.

Several factors seem to militate for the continued use of Amharic. The available manpower is one case in point. All those who are capable of teaching can do so in Amharic, because they are themselves the product of the school system that teaches Amharic and in Amharic as well. The idea of using other languages is frustrated because the needed manpower is not available for some. For others, it may not be adequate or available at the site where it is most needed. In most bilingual situations, most towns, factories, the army, the police force, state farms, etc., Amharic is the preferred medium. Some participants also seem to favor Amharic to their first tongues. Those who are motivated to continue their studies beyond the literacy level need to know Amharic, because from that point on, education is provided in Amharic. For those who would like to go beyond the bounds of their communities looking for better opportunities, Amharic is particularly attractive.

3.3.4 The mass media

The mass media, an aspect of modernization, has also been instrumental for the extended use and spread of Amharic. From the start, the primary medium of the media, destined for a national audience, has been Amharic. As such, the two have developed to the same extent.

In Ethiopia, the first weekly, an Amharic-French medium, appeared in Harar in 1890. Two years later, *Ayimro*, and three years after that *Atbia Kokeb*, both Amharic weeklies, began circulating in Addis Ababa (Abdu 1976:505). With the advent of the printing press, their circulation greatly increased. However, the real impact of print media came about when the Department of Press and Information, later a ministry, was established in 1941, and the media as an important arm of a modernizing state apparatus was recognized.

The dailies, weeklies and other periodicals that began to appear in regular fashion and in large numbers are in Amharic. In addition, those branches of the government that needed to have their own papers also chose Amharic as a medium. The Armed Forces have their own Amharic weeklies. The police force has a popular national paper too. Regional towns that were able to have their own papers, like Harar and Gondar, did the same. Except for Tigrigna and most recently Oromo, no other native tongue is used in print media. The Tigrigna paper, one of the oldest, has a limited circulation and serves the Asomera area only.

The overall story in the oral media is not any different. The main tongue of television broadcasting is Amharic. The daily evening news, news analysis and some social programs are all conducted in Amharic. If and when government decrees or directives are issued, the medium is Amharic. In radio broadcasting some other Ethiopian languages are used, but to a limited extent. In recent years, however, their use has been increased substantially. According to the 1979 program, close to half (43.3%) of the broadcasting time has been allocated to these language services. Oromo language programs run 18.52% of the total; Tigrigna for 13.89%; Somali, Tigre and Afar each for 4.63% of the total time. Amharic language programs accounted for 37.50% of the time. The rest was allocated to English, French, and Arabic language programs. Measures like this could be considered as part of the overall effort to "correct the weakness of the previous radio broadcasting which has missed its logical audience" (Abdu 1976:507). There is also an effort to establish regional stations like those in Harar and Asmera to ensure the continued use of these languages. The educational services in various regional tongues is also promising in this regard.

As the uses of various regional tongues increases, a new pattern of language function in radio broadcasting seems to be emerging. More and more, the regional tongues seem to concentrate on purposes that are mainly of regional and local importance, while Amharic tends to be used for those that are national. This diglossic relationship may help create the conditions and the attitude for the continued use and diffusion of Amharic in rural Ethiopia.

3.4 Amharic as a **biherawi quanqua**

The use of the term **biherawi quanqua** (National Language) in reference to Amharic is a recent phenomenon. It dates back to the 1960's. By the early 1970's, the media and other public institutions had begun to use it freely and routinely.

The term **national language** is used here to refer to languages that function at the supra-ethnic level in multilingual socities. In this regard, national languages are common tongues, but they are more than that. They have a symbolic function, which they attained as a result of higher social developments achieved in their respective societies. With the rise of capitalism—urbanization, industrialization, commercialization, mass means of communication and attendant sociocultural progress—the narrow ethnic boundaries began to break. Consequently, the various regions became interdependent making contact among the ethnic groups regular and extensive and a necessary aspect of their life. In fact, many people were drawn from various parts of the country and came to work in the factories, live in the cities, and send their children to the same schools. That gave rise to a new and common culture. As part of the overall transformation of society, one of the tongues evolved and became not only a common tongue, but also a symbol of the emerging common identity—the nation.

The particular case of Ethiopia is different from this. Ethiopia is a developing country. The level of its urbanization, industrialization, and commercialization of its economy is very low. That is, the material conditions that could have brought its various groups closer together are accordingly weak. In spite of all this, however, there has been a growing aspiration for nationhood in the country.

The beginning of this aspiration can be traced back to the middle of the last century when Ethiopia was suddenly awakened from its long isolation and found that its sovereignty was seriously threatened. The threat was so real that it arounsed great concern among the various regional leaders of the time. Cognizant of the impending danger, these leaders were each engaged in seeking ways and means of establishing and maintaining strong defences. In the civil war that followed, they allied and reallied and fought against each other until at last Tewodros emerged victorious. Thus, the history of modern Ethiopia began (Rubenson 1976, 1984).

Tewodros' (1855–68) primary aim was to establish "a united, strong and progressive Ethiopian state" (Rubenson 1976:71). For various reasons he did not accomplish what he set out to achieve. Although his success was limited, his reign has become significant, because "it initiated the unification and modernization process by revealing the problems involved and making the first attempt to find solutions" (Rubenson 1976:76). What is even more significant is the legacy that was created after him and which has captured the imaginations of poets, dramatists and novelists. For many Ethiopians he is a national hero and a resolute and determined defender of the country. His tragic death has also become part of the legend and seems to have advanced national unity and independence. Among the educated, he is a farsighted leader who earnestly fought against traditionalism and for modernization. His modest family background has been particularly inspirational to the group which has come to subscribe to an "achieved" status as opposed to an "ascribed" one.

The sucessors of Tewodros had inherited his vision along with the throne. Confronted with the same sort of problems, they were primarily engaged in maintaining national unity, which they did. They were thus able to frustrate the ambitions of the country's enemies time and again. For example, Yohannes IV and his generals defeated the Italians, Turks, and Egyptians on several occasions. Yohannes' death, like that of Tewodros' before him, has strengthened the national unity, because he too died while defending the country. Seven years later, Manlik II scored a decisive victory over the Italians in a major war and was able to maintain the national independence and advance the unity even further.

Menlik's victory was significant in many ways. Internationally, Ethiopia was able to secure its place among the community of nations. Menlik's government was recognized by several foreign powers, who estabished their consulates in Addis Ababa. Soon after, they sent their representatives to Addis Ababa in order "to negotiate treaties, demarcate borders, establish commercial relations and gain concessions" (Markakis 1974:144). For his part, Manlik defined the extent and limits of his country and made it known to all concerned. On the home front, his victory had even more significance. Out of the war came a united Ethiopia. The various regional leaders not only fought under him but also came to recognize his authority. They became part of the building of the new state. His capital, the new commercial and cultural center of the country, began to attract promising people from various parts of the country including Eritrea which was then under Italian colonial rule (S. Pankhurst 1955). This group along with the modern educated people became the architects of the emerging state. The modern state apparatus which he was able to institute eventually became an important instrument for the dissemination of the idea of belonging to one nation. This has been particularly true in recent years. During Haile Sellasie's reign, a relatively high degree of institutionalization and centralization of political authority has been acheived because of the lesson learned and because the people who run the system are better educated than were their predecessors.

Modern education, by its nature and function, has even been a more consistent and systematic agent of the diffusion of the notion of nationhood in Ethiopia. Right from the start the new schools were established with the expressed purpose "to promote pride in Ethiopia's freedom and independence, and in the maintenance, honoured and respected, of her frontiers as well as to produce a confident firmness in the hearts of her people" (Pankhurst 1962:266). To that effect the regional leaders were urged to open and support such schools and send their children also. To do so was viewed as a token of one's own devotion and love to the country (Pankhurst 1962).

As could be expected, the graduates of these schools have willingly accepted the responsibility and challenge of advancing the causes of unity, modernization, and maintenance of national sovereignty. We need educated people," declared Ashebr G. Hiwot, one of the early educated Ethiopians, "in order to ensure our peace, to reconstruct our country and to enable it to exist as a great nation in the face of European nations" (cited in Pankhurst 1962:256). Both in time of peace and war they stood together and for the good of their country. Before and during the Italian invasion (1936–41), they used every means at their disposal to raise the consciousness of the people and to organize them to fight against the enemy. Their heroism was such that the Italians were so alarmed that they "singled out this group for special savage treatment" (Markakis 1974:146). All this did not deter them. If any thing, the Italian invasion had "helped to stimulate a new sense of Ethiopian nationalism" (Clapham 1984:461). It also helped to break down the local autonomy further, making the various patriotic leaders, who were more traditional in their orientation and regional in their politics, bearers of national independence and unity (Clapham 1984).

In their struggle against tradition and the forces of reaction within the country, educated Ethiopians have also advanced national unity and modernization. In their effort to educate the populace, they earned the enmity of the nobility and clergy. Using popular literature as a means, they exposed the sources of ignorance, poverty and degradation of the people. In their writings "there is an overt critique of Ethiopian society and mores. All emphasize, in varying degrees, the need to abolish the exorbitant principles of the feudal lords, to outgrow obsolete superstition and degraded custom, to accept technological change" (Gerard 1971:303).

In dealing with issues of national concern, educated Ethiopians managed to develop a national literature in Amharic. The development of the national literature, in its turn, helps to "itimate that Ethiopia's official language is being increasingly recognized as a genuine national lingua franca and cultural tongue" (Gerard 1971:355). For the most part, the educated have served "the cause of unity, because their parochial loyalties are suppressed by their loyalties to a progressive and united Ethiopia" (Abraham 1969).

The other factor that has promoted the national awareness is the country's increasing contact with the outside world. Since Ethiopia emerged from its isolation, its international relations have steadily grown. It was a member of the League of Nations and has been a member of the United Nations since its inception. It is also a founding member of the Organization of African Unity and Non-aligned Nations. Addis Ababa is the headquarters of the OAU and the Economic Commission for Africa. Consequently, the city's international community is growing. In addition, Ethiopians have also begun to travel abroad on a variety of missions. Thus, through various means, Ethiopians are presented with the opportunity to compare and contrast their society and culture with those of others. Therefore, a growing number of them have become overtly critical of their government and society. At the same time, these same contacts have enabled them to appreciate some of what they have. Among these sources of national pride is the fact that the national language is indigenous and their literary heritage is the product of native effort and ingenuity. As Levine remarked, "even among those who are not Amharic speakers, those who are aware of the situation elsewhere in Africa tend to take pride in the fact that their national language is indigenous, not as is true in most other African countries an alien tongue" (cited in Gerald 1971:355).

The momentum of the building of Ethiopia's nationhood seems to have reached its peak in the 1960's. In the area of language use and status this was spelled out in the efforts of some people who attempted to strengthen the national status of Amharic. The proponents were unorganized but were comprised of individuals from various ethnic groups and professions, and some were members of the *National Language Academy* who had initiated public discussion in the media. The discussion focused on the symbolic functions of Amharic. It was believed that the name Amharic was not a facilitating factor. In fact, "Amharic" was considered an inappropriate name for a national language because of its affiliation with the name of one of the ethnic groups—the Amhara. It was argued that the name of the national language should be neutral and should be free of any sectarian connotation. Thus, an all inclusive name, Ityopyawigna (Ethiopia) was suggested as a solution. The rational was that with a neutral name, the national language would become truely national. It was also hoped that the neutral name would serve as an integrating and unifying factor (Hailu, personal communication).

Since the Revolution, however, the policy as well as the general perception towards the notion of "national language" have changed. In fact, with the promulgation of the National Democratic Revolution Program (1976), all languages are accorded equal status. Amharic does not have official status anymore. Nevertheless, it has continued to be used in the various domains and for even more occasions and purposes than before, because the Revolution has opened more opportunities for its use. Amharic publications have increased both in kind and number. On the other hand, its symbolic function has been limited. Despite its extended use, the promotion of Amharic to national language status is not officially sanctioned. In the Draft Constitution (1986), however, it is recognized as the working language of the government of Ethiopia.

3.5 Why an indegeneous tongue was chosen

It has so far been argued that along with the modernization and unification of the country, the need for a common tongue arose and that need was met by Amharic. One wonders why Ethiopia did not choose one of the tongues—English, French, or Italian—that best suited the purpose of modernization. One may even argue that the purpose of unification would have been better achieved if any one of these tongues were used because they were equally alien to all ethnic groups in the country thus denying privileged status to all groups alike.

The answer to this question may be found in the particular history of Ethiopia. As Levine (1974) remarked, "the Ethiopian state represents an historic nation which has largely preserved its own institutions, elites and cultures from displacement by Western forms of authorities." Thus, from its advent, modernization (institutions, materials, and know-how) was not destined to replace old values altogether but to supplement them. In contrast to other countries, in Ethiopia the overall decision as to what and how much innovation was needed was the prerogative of the national forces. For the most part, external forces were limited to advisory capacities. Their presence and degree of influence were therefore checked to a considerable extent. Besides, the foreign forces were of varied national origin with differing and conflicting interests. They were often jealous of each other's success to the extent of impeding each other's progress. This enabled the national forces to better control and at times even manipulate the foreign forces to their own advantages (Pankhurst 1962, Aleme 1973). Consequently, no one external force was able to make the desired impact for its language to become a lingua franca or an official tongue in Ethiopia.

The indegenous forces that could have prompted any one of these tongues to official status were at first weak and divided. In fact, at the time when the crucial steps were taken, this group did not exist as a viable political force. In time, its strength and influence may have grown but never to the extent of becoming a contender to political power. The local force's independent political existence has only recently begun. In the past, it existed as an appendage to one or another of the traditional forces. From the start, it was divided into factions. One group was comprised of educated French and the other educated English people with no desire or ability to assume political power. The contention between them was such that it seems to have adversely affected the success of one or the other group.

Above all, at the time when the need for a common tongue

was growing, the forces associated with foreign tongues had no influence in the country. They were also generally perceived as adversaries. The attempt of some to colonize the country was current then and deeply resented. The Portuguese missionaries' venture to convert the people to their faith, which plunged the country into a civil war, was not yet forgotten. This was especially true among the clergy and the nobility, a formidable power block that was not particularly appreciative of the idea of modernization and change in the first place. In fact, the continued intervention of these foreign forces had precipitated the rise of national awareness among the people and strong suspicion towards foreigners.

However, it should be noted that the country has been appreciative of the progress made by the foreign forces. Consequently, its desire was great to acquire their languages as vehicles of science and technology which were badly needed. But Ethiopia seems to have reserved the right to be selective of what it wanted to take. In the schools, for example, foreign languages began to be taught and/or used as the media of instruction early on. Nevertheless, the learning of Amharic and Geez was not excluded. In principle, the learning of the native tongues was considered an important component of nation-building and a necessary prerequisite for the learning of the foreign languages and the skills and know-how through them (Pankhurst 1962).

With the advent and expansion of modernization and attendant culture, institutions and social organizations, the use of foreign languages, especially English, has steadily grown. English is now the only medium of instruction for the secondary schools and the institutes of higher education. The country conducts its international trade and diplomacy in English. Outside such specialized domains, the impact of English is very limited. A new diglossic relationship has thus been created between Amharic and English. English is used in scientific, technical, and international domains, while Amharic is used in those that are national, official, and formal.

In some ways, the position that English has come to occupy is comparable to the one Geez previously held. Just like Geez before it, English is not used outside some specialized domains. If the people involved are all Ethiopians, irrespective of their ethnic composition, the medium preferred for oral discourse is Amharic. It is not uncommon for professional Ethiopians to discuss the matter of their concern in Amharic and write the re´sult in English. Even among professionals, one who tends to use English among fellow Ethiopians is hardly appreciated, although a good command of English is highly valued but only when used appropriately.

No foreign tongue, including English, has been made available to the people at large. English is the widely used foreign tongue but has not become a contact language in the country. It is not used for everyday purposes by any group, and there are no native speakers. Except for a few specialized agencies, English is not used in government administration either. A very large part of the bureaucracy either does not know it or does not have a good command of the language. Thus, the conditions have never been conducive for the introduction of a foreign tongue to become a common medium in Ethiopia.

4. Summary and conclusion

Modernization is not a total success story in Ethiopia. A lot remains to be desired, but progress is being made. In contrast to its past, modern Ethiopia has made certain strides which have altered the statuses and functions of its various tongues. The structure and functions of its state apparatus are more institutionalised and continue to be so. Modern public education is increasingly made available to a growing number of people and in various parts of the country. The impact of the market economy is being felt by more and more people. Urban centers are mushrooming throughout the coutry and are influencing the regions around them. Mass means of transportation have made travel within the country relatively easy. Consequently, in present-day Ethiopia, the reasons for and the means through which interethnic contacts are made have become steady and extensive. It is because of these reasons that the need for a common medium has arisen, and it is in accordance with these needs that the diffusion of the common medium has been realized.

Today, unlike in traditional Ethiopia, all those who have access to political power also have access to the medium of the government they intend to replace. Thus, there is no compelling reason or practical need to change the language of government whenever one government is replaced by another. As a matter of fact, the odds are against change. The structure and functions of the government have now become sufficiently complex to require the continued use of the common tongue. The national elite that is increasingly needed to run the bureaucracy and such other national institutions has developed vested interest in the continued use of the common tongue. The fact that Amharic is that medium is an accident of history. Whatever the language is, there is a need for a common tongue in the country.

At the initial stage, the dominance of some languages over others in multilingual societies is attributed, primarily, to the hierarchical nature of their social systems. In Ethiopia, the state with the Niguse Negest (King of Kings) at its head had existed for over two millenia. Consequently, it was the languages that were associated with the persons and institutions of power, authority and corresponding social prestige that attained prominence early on. Once that association is attained, it becomes a factor in itself for the continued dominance of that tongue over others. Amharic, which was spoken in a rather compact area in what is now the Wellow Administrative Region, by the beginning of this millenium began to spread out as soon as it bacame a Lisane Nigus (King's tongue) (Taddesse 1972). Early on, it spread to the adjoining regions of Gojjam, Gondar, Shewa, and Wello. These are now generally referred to as traditional Amharic-speaking regions. Because of its privileged status, it was gradually introduced as the auxiliary medium of religion and education and has eventually become the primary medium of writing. Now it is a relatively more developed and standardized language with an extensive literary heritage appealing to a growing number of people. As the working language of the government (the largest employer), the school system, and other national institutions, Amharic is also closely associated with better opportunities. It is thus gaining ground among the young and educated generation. In general, bilingualism in Amharic is steadily on the rise. The revolutionary reorganization of the Ethiopian society and the change in its language policy does not seem to affect this general trend.

In Ethiopia "the single lingua franca" (Greenberg 1966: 52) may be in the making. However, as things now stand, the factors are not sufficienty strong for the process to be consummated. That is, before Amharic becomes a truely common tongue, it must serve the urban as well as the rural, the center as well the periphery. It must also attain a higher level of development. For all these to happen, the country as a whole has to attain a higher level of socioeconomic and cultural development. Secondly, the type of language policy that the state will choose to follow will also be important in this regard. The prevailing conditions dictate that the policy be pluralistic in orientation and democratic in approach. The practice of promoting Amharic as a common/national tongue at the expense of other languages, as in the past, will only have adverse consequences. Therefore, it is imperative that the policy account for the needs of the people associated with the uses of local, national and international languages. Along with the overall social development, it is democratic social practices that will ensure the further development of the common/national language in Ethiopia, as in other developing countries.

Selected Bibliography

Abdul Mozayen. 1976. "The Use of the Mass Media in Language Teaching." In: M. L. Bender, ed. *Language in Ethiopia*. Oxford: Oxford University Press, 505–519.

Abir, Mordechia. 1969. *Ethiopia: The Era of the Princes*. New York: Praeger.

Abir, Mordechia. 1975. "Ethiopia and the Horn of Africa." In *The Cambridge History of Africa*. Vol. 4, 537–577. Edited by K. Gray. Cambridge University Press.

Abir, Mordechia. 1980. *Ethiopia and the Red Sea: The Rise and Decline of the Solomonic Dynasty and Muslim-European Rivalary in the Region*. London: Frank Cass.

Abraham, Demoz. 1968. "Amharic for Modern Use." *The Ethiopian Journal of Education*. 2: 1: 15–29.

Abraham, Demoz. 1969. "The Many Worlds of Ethiopia." *African Affairs* 68: 270, 49–54.

Abraham, Demoz. 1970. "Language Modernization in Ethiopia." A paper presented at the Language Association of Eastern Africa Conference on Language for Development in Eastern Africa.

Abraham, Demoz. 1973. "Language and Society in Ethiopia." *Institut für Auslandsbeziehungen und für Kulturaustausch Sonderausgabe: Äthiopien*. Stuttgart.

Abraham, Demoz. 1978. "Ethiopian Origins: A Survey." *Abbay* 9: 11–14. Centre Nationale de le Recherche Scientifique.

Akalou, W. Michael. 1973. "Urban Development in Ethiopia (1889–1925)." *Journal of Ethiopian Studies*. 11: 1: 1–16.

Aleme Eshete. 1973. "The Role and Position of Foreign-Educated Interpreters in Ethiopia (1880–1889)." *Journal of Ethiopian Studies*. Vol XI. No. 1.

Aleme Eshete. 1974. "The Pre-War Attempts to Promote the Use of the English Language in the Educational System of Ethiopia in Place of French." *The Ethiopian Journal of Education*. 6: 2: 15–29.

Bender, Marvin L. 1971. "The Languages of Ethiopia: A New Lexico- Statistic Classification and Some Problems of Diffusion." *Anthropological Linguistics*. 13: 5: 165–284.

Bender, Marvin. 1975. *Omotic: A New Afroasiatic Language Family*. Southern Illinois Museum Series. No. 3.

Bender, Marvin. 1976. *The Non-Semitic Languages of Ethiopia*. East Lansing: African Studies Center, Michigan University Press.

Bender, Marvin et. al. 1976. *Language in Ethiopia*. London: Oxford University Press.

Bright, William. 1966. *Sociolinguistics*. The Hague: Mouton.

Brosnahan, L. F. 1963. "Some Historical Cases of Language Imposition." In: R. Spencer, ed. *Language in Africa*. London: Cambridge University Press, 7–24.

Brown, J. Donald. 1976. "Historical Background of Education in Ethiopia." In: M. L. Bender, ed. *Language in Ethiopia*, Oxford: Oxford University Press, 305–323.

Bruce, James. 1964. *Travels to Discover the Source of the Nile*. Selected and edited by C. F. Beckingham. Edinburgh University Press.

Budge, E. W. 1928. *A History of Ethiopia: Nubia and Abyssinia*. London: Methuen.

Central Statistical Office (CSO). 1977. *Analysis of Demographic Data of Urban Areas Covered During Urban Survey Second Round 1969–1971*. Addis Ababa: Central Printing Press.

Central Statistical Office. 1978. *Ethiopia: Statistical Abstract*. Addis Ababa: Central Printing Press.

Central Statistical Office. 1980. *Ethiopia: Statistical Abstract*. Addis Ababa: Central Printing Press.

Chittick, Nevile. 1978. "Notes on the Archeology of Northern Ethiopia." *Abbay*, 15–20. Centre Nationale de la Recherche Scientifique.

Clapham, Christopher. 1984. "The Horn of Africa." *The Cambridge History of Africa: From 1940 to 1975*. London: Cambridge University Press.

Conti Rossini, C. 1935. *Storia d'Etiopia*. Milano: Officina d'dite grafica A. Lucini.

Cooper, Robert L. 1970. "The Description of Language Use in Ethiopia." *Journal of the Language Association of Eastern Ethiopia*. 1: 1: 6–10.

Cooper, Robert L. 1976 a. "Government Language Policy." In: M. L. Bender, ed. *Language in Ethiopia*. Oxford: Oxford University Press, 187–190.

Cooper, Robert L. 1976 b. "The Spread of Amharic." In: *Language in Ethiopia*, 289–304.

Cooper, Robert L. 1979. "Language Planning, Language Spread and Language Change." In: J. E. Alatis, G. R. Tucker, eds. *Georgetown University Round Table on Languages and Linguistics 1979*. Washington, D.C.: Georgetown University Press, 23–50.

Cooper, Robert L. and S. Carpenter. 1969. "Linguistic Diversity in the Ethiopian Market." *Journal of African Languages* 8:23: 160–68.

Cooper, Robert L. and E. Horvath. 1976. "Language Migration and Urbanization in Ethiopia." In: M. L. Bender, ed. *Language in Ethiopia*. Oxford: Oxford University Press, 168–185.

Cooper, Robert L. and Fasil Nahum. 1976. "Language in the Court." In: M. L. Bender, ed. *Language in Ethiopia*. Oxford: Oxford University Press, 256–263.

Cooper, Robert L., B. N. Singh and Abrham G. Zion. 1976. "Mother Tongues and other Tongues in Keffa and Arusi." In: M. L. Bender, ed. *Language in Ethiopia*. Oxford: Oxford University Press, 213–243.

Cooper, Robert L. and B. N. Singh. 1976. "Language and Factory Workers." In: M. L. Bender, ed. *Language in Ethiopia*. Oxford: Oxford University Press, 246–272.

Cooper, Robert L. and K. Michael. 1976. "Language and University Students." In: M. L. Bender, ed. *Language in Ethiopia*. Oxford: Oxford University Press, 273–280.

Darkwah, R. H. 1975. *Shewa, Menilk and the Ethiopian Empire 1813–1889*. London: Heineman Educational. Deutsch, K. W. 1968. "The Trend of European Nationalism: The Language Aspect." In: J. A. Fishman, ed. *Readings in the Sociology of Language*. The Hague: Mouton, 598–606.

Deutsch, K.W. 1953. *Nationalism and Social Communication: An Inquiry into the Foundations of Nationality*. The M.I.T. Press.

Ferguson, C. A. 1959. "Diglossia." *Word*. 15: 325–340.

Ferguson, C. A. 1966. "National Sociolinguistic Formulas." In: W. Bright, ed. *Sociolinguistics*. The Hague: Mouton, 309–324.

Ferguson, C. A. 1970."The Role of Arabic in Ethiopia: A Sociolinguistic Perspective." In: *Language Structure and Use*. Essays by C.A. Ferguson. Selected and Introduced by A.S. Dill. Stanford: Standford University Press.

Ferguson, C. A. 1976. "The Ethiopian Language Area." In: *Language in Ethiopia*, 63–76.

Fishman, J. A. 1972. *Language and Nationalism: Two Integrative Essays*. Rowley, MA: Newbury House Publishers.

Fleming, H. C. 1968. "Ethiopian Language History: Testing Linguistic Hypothesis in an Archeological and Documentary Context." *Ethnohistory*. 15: 533–388.

Gerard, Albert C. 1968. "Amharic Creative Literature: The Early Phase."*Journal of Ethiopian Studies*, 6: 2: 39–59.

Gerard, Albert C. 1971.*Four African Literatures*. Berkeley: University of California Press.

Getachew, Haile. 1968. "Amarigna Lemin Yeityopya Quanqua Hone?" *Dialogue*. 2: 2: 76–81.

Getachew, Haile. Ms. "Some Notes on the History of Ethiopia: A Re-examination of the Documents." A paper presented at Quo Vadis Ethiopia, November 1982. Howard University.

Greenberg, J.H. 1966. *The Languages of Africa*. Indiana University Press.

Guxman, M. M. 1968. "Some General Regularities in the Formation and Development of National Languages." In: J. A. Fishman, ed. *Readings in the Sociology of Language.*The Hague: Mouton: 766–779.

Habte Mariam Marcos. 1973. "Regional Variation in Amharic." *Journal of Ethiopian Studies.* 11: 2: 112–129.

Haile G. Dagne. 1976. "Non-Government Schools in Ethiopia." In: M. L. Bender, ed. *Language in Ethiopia.* Oxford: Oxford University Press, 339–370.

Hailu Fulas et. al. 1976. "The Amharic Language: Dialect Variation." In: *Language in Ethiopia,* 90–98.

Hudson, Grover. 1977. "Language Classification and the Semitic Prehistory of Ethiopia." *Folia Oriekalia.* 18: 119–166.

Hudson, Grover. 1978. "Geolinguistic Evidence for Ethiopian Semitic Prehistory." *Abbay.* 4: 71–85. Centre Nationale de la Recherche Scientifique.

Imperial Ethiopian Government. 1972. "National Academy of the Amharic Language." *Negarit Gazeta.* 1972: 126–131. ·

Irvine, A. K. 1965. "On the Identity of the Habashat in the South Arabian Inscriptions." *Journal of Semitic Studies.* 10: 178–196.

Jones, A.H.M. and Monroe, E. 1971. *A History of Abyssinia.* Oxford: The Clarendon Press.

Korten, D. C. 1972. *Planned Change in an Traditional Society: Psychological Problems of Modernization in Ethiopia.* New York: Praeger Publishers.

Lambert, W. E. 1967. "The Social Psychology of Bilingualism." *Journal of Social Issues.* 23: 91–109.

Le Page, R. B. 1964. *The National Language Question: Linguistic Problems of Newly Independent States.* London: Oxford University Press.

Leslau, Wolf. 1958. "The Languages of Ethiopia and Their Geographical Distribution." *Ethiopia Observer.* 2/3: 110–121.

Levine, Donald N. 1965. "Ethiopia: Identity, Authority and Realism." In: L. Pye and S. Verba, eds. *Political Culture and Political Development.* Princeton University Press.

Levine, Donald N. 1971. "The Roots of Ethiopia's Nationhood." *Africa Report.* 16: 5: 12–14.

Levine, Donald N. 1974. *Greater Ethiopia: The Evolution of Multiethnic Society.* Chicago University Press.

Lieberson, Stanley. 1982. "Forces Affecting Language Spread: Some Basic Propositions." In: R. L. Cooper, ed. *Language Spread: Studies in Diffusion and Social Change* Bloomington, IN: Indiana University Press, 37–62.

Ludolf, H. 1982. *A New History of Ethiopia.* London: S. Smith. Marcus, Harold G. 1975. *The Life and Times of Menelik II: Ethiopia 1844–1913.* Oxford: Clarendon Press.

Markakis, John. 1974. *Ethiopia: Anatomy of a Traditional Polity.* Oxford: Clarendon Press.

Merid W. Aregay. 1974. "Political Geography of Ethiopia at the Beginning of the Sixteenth Century." *IV Congresso Internazionale di Studi Etiopic, Tomo I,* pp. 613–631. Roma Accadamia Nazionale dei Lincei.

NDR. 1976. *National Democratic Revolution Program of Ethiopia.* Addis Ababa: Central Printing Press.

Negarit Gazeta. 1972. "National Academy of the Amharic Language." Establishment Order No. 79 of 1972.

Pankhurst, E. S. 1955. *Ethiopia: A Cultural History*. Essex: Lalibela House.

Pankhurst, Richard. 1962. "The Foundations of Education, Printing, Newspapers, Book Production, Libraries and Literature in Ethiopia." *Ethiopia Observer*. 6: 241–290.

Pankhurst, Richard. 1974. "Education, Language and History: An Historical Background to Post-War Ethiopia." *The Ethiopian Journal of Education*. 7: 1: 75–97.

Pankhurst, Richard. 1976. "Historical Background of Education in Ethiopia." In: M. L. Bender, ed. *Language in Ethiopia*. Oxford: Oxford University Press, 305–323.

PMAC. 1974. *Ethiopia Tikdem*. Declaration of the Provisional Military Government of Ethiopia. Addis Ababa.

PMAC. 1983. *The Institute for the Study of Ethiopian Nationalities*. Declaration of the Provisional Military Government of Ethiopia. Addis Ababa.

Revised Constitution of Ethiopia. 1955. *Negarit Gazeta: Proclamation No. 149*, Article 125.

Richter, Renate. Ms. "Some Aspects of Bi- and Multilingualism in the Context of National Consolidation."

Rubenson, S. 1968. *The Survival of Ethiopian Independence*. London: Heineman Educational Books.

Rubenson, S. 1976. "Ethiopia and the Horn." In *The Cambridge History of Africa*, Vol. 5, 51–98. Edited by J.E. Flint. Cambridge University Press.

Taddesse, Tamirat. 1972. *Church and State in Ethiopia 1270–1527*. Oxford: Clarendon Press.

Taddesse, Tamirat. 1977. "Ethiopia, the Red Sea and the Horn." In: *The Cambridge History of Africa*. 3: 99–182. Edited by R. Oliver. Cambridge University Press.

Trimingham, J. Spencer. 1952. *Islam in Ethiopia*. London: Oxford University Press.

Ullendorff, Edward. 1960. *The Ethiopians: An Introduction to People and Country*. London: Oxford University Press.

Zewdie G. Sellasie. 1975. *Yohannes IV of Ethiopia: A Political Biography*. Oxford: Clarendon Press.

Malay in Indonesia, Malaysia, and Singapore: Three Faces of a National Language

Peter H. Lowenberg

Introduction

Contemporary Indonesia, Malaysia, and Singapore provide excellent examples of the diverse rationales for the adoption of a national language and for the consequences and implications of selecting a particular language for this role. For unlike other contexts in which national language policies have been compared, these countries afford a rare opportunity to analyze several sociolinguistic variables operating on a common national language, Malay, in a contiguous geographic area that has been influenced since prehistory by similar linguistic and nonlinguistic developments.

For the half millenium prior to the colonial era, this region shared Malay as a lingua franca for basically identical functions associated with maritime trade. However, significant differences in the colonial and post-colonial experiences of these countries have caused substantial divergence in their respective motives for and the sociolinguistic impact of their selection of Malay as a national language. In this survey of the national language question in these countries, I will review the historical role of the Malay language in the area, discuss the diverse reasons why Malay was selected as the sole national language in these countries, and examine the results of this solution to the national language question in all three nations.

Pre-colonial Era

The region comprising present-day Indonesia, Malaysia, and Singapore has always been unified in terms of its indigenous languages, most of which share phonological, morphosyntactic, and lexical features marking them as members of the Western Indonesian sub-branch of the Malayo-Polynesian language family (Dyen 1971; Voegelin and Voegelin 1964).

These linguistic bonds are further consolidated by the use of one of these languages, Malay, since prehistory as the primary lingua franca of the region. As Alisjahbana observes (1976:32),

> because the extensive area of Indonesia and Malaysia is fragmented into hundreds of geographical, cultural, and most important, linguistic units, there has been from time immemorial a need for a single common language which could be understood not only by the natives of the archipelago but also by the constant waves of foreigners attracted by celebrated riches.

Malay's assumption of this role has resulted from its long use as a mother tongue on both the Sumatran and Malay sides of the Straits of Malacca, which have continually been the keystone to maritime commerce in Southeast Asia. The Malay inhabitants of this area have always been active traders and navigators, spreading their language with them at all their ports of call (Gonda 1973). Concurrently, "traders, migrants, and even pirates who plied up and down the Straits of Malacca could not escape contact with Malay-speaking people" (Asmah 1982:202–203), whose language they subsequently learned and then used in their interethnic contacts with one another.

The first institutionalized spread of Malay occurred during the Srivijaya Empire (seventh through fourteenth centuries A.D.), which adopted Malay as its official language. From its capital at

Table 1 (adapted from Nababan 1985:4)
Major and Some Secondary Languages in Indonesia

No	Language	Location (Concentration)	No. of Speakers (in Thousands)
1.	Indonesian (Bahasa Indonesia)	Whole country	17,640 **
2.	Javanese	Central & East Java	58,855 **
3.	Sundanese	West Java	22.385 **
4.	Malay dialects	General areas in Sumatra & Kalimantan	13,745 **
5.	Madurese	Madura and East Java	7,057 **
6.	Bugis/Makasar	South Celebes	2,811 **
7.	Minangkabau	West Sumatra	3,705 **
8.	Batak	North Central Sumatra	3,122 **
9.	Balinese	Bali	2,994 **
10.	Achenese	Aceh	1,750 *
11.	Sasak	Lombok Sumbawa	1,576 *
12.	Mandar	South Celebes	787 *
13.	Minahasa	North Celebes	777 *
14.	Gorontalo	North Celebes	490 *
15.	Halmahera	Halmahera	372
16.	Nias	Nias (North Sumatra)	461 *
17.	Sangsir/Talaud	North Celebes	407 *
18.	Toraja (Southern)	South Celebes	393 *
19.	Bima	East Sumbawa	375 *
20.	Buton (Butung)	Southeast Celebes	372 *
21.	Sumba	Sumba	359 *
22.	Sumbawa	West Sumbawa	300 *
23.	Manggarai	Flores	272 *
24.	Bolaang Mangondow	North Celebes	260 *
25.	Rejang Lebong	West South Sumatra	256 *
26.	Gayo/Alas	Central Aceh	248 *
27.	Sikka	Flores	221 *
28.	Kerinci	South Central Sumatra	230 *
29.	Ende	Flores	221 *
30.	Muna	Maluku (Moluccas)	190 *
31.	Ngada	Flores	178 *
32.	Kai	Maluku (Moluccas)	133 *

Notes: * Estimated on basis of 1971 census; no figures in 1980 census
          ** As given in preliminary tables of 1980 census

contemporary Palembang in southern Sumatra and a secondary base at Kedah on the Malay Peninsula, Srivijaya eventually conquered all of Sumatra, West and Central Java, and the Malay Peninsula, establishing colonies along all seacoasts and major rivers within its domain. It maintained diplomatic relations with both India and China and effectively controlled both the Straits of

Malacca and the Straits of Sunda (between Sumatra and Java) for over five centuries (Cady 1964; Harrison 1967; Williams 1976). The extensive area over which Malay had official status during the Srivijaya era is reflected by the widespread locations of stone monuments with Malay inscriptions in Devanagari script later found on Sumatra, Java, and the Malay Peninsula (Alisjahbana 1976; Asmah 1982). In addition to its use within the actual political domains of Srivijaya, Gonda (1973:87) surmises that the empire "in all probability, likewise furthered the spread of Malay over adjacent countries which felt its influence."

The decline from power of Srivijaya by no means lessened the role of Malay. For with the subsequent expansion of the Islamic kingdom of Malacca during the fifteenth century, the Malay spoken by sailors from the smaller islands in and around the Straits of Malacca—a variety slightly different from that used in Srivijaya—continued the tradition of Malay as a lingua franca in the Archipelago (Abas 1978; Williams 1976). Furthermore, Malay became the language of proselytization by Muslim missionaries who followed the trade routes and brought the language into greater contact with present-day Indonesia (Gonda 1973).

By the time the first Europeans arrived, Malay was well-established as the only lingua franca in the Archipelago (Teeuw 1967). Pigafetta, who accompanied Magellan on his first circumnavigation of the world, compiled the first Portuguese-Malay glossary in 1521 while harbored at Tidore, one of the far eastern Indonesian islands, which is indicative of just how far Malay had spread. Soon afterward, St. Francis Xavier is quoted as having referred to Malay as "the language that everyone understands," and in 1614, Jan Huygen van Linschoten, a Dutch navigator, observed that "Malay was not merely known but was also considered the most prestigious of the languages of the Orient . . . he who did not understand it was in somewhat the same position as Dutchmen of the period who did not understand French" (Alisjahbana 1976:33–34).

Colonial Indonesia

With the advent of the colonial era, differences between the objectives and policies of the British in Malaya and those of the

Dutch in the Netherlands East Indies became reflected in greatly divergent status and functions of Malay in these colonies. The Dutch colonization of present-day Indonesia (1600–1942) was extremely conducive to the expanded use of Malay. Unlike the British, discussed below, the Dutch strove for monopolistic control in Indonesia and carefully guarded against foreign intrusions on their largely plantation economy. In particular, they severely restricted immigration of other Asians, resulting in a population which was almost entirely indigenous to the islands and which had long shared Malay as a link language.

Although Dutch was initially the only official colonial language, the Dutch themselves found Malay extremely useful as an auxiliary language for local administration and for communication with the linguistically diverse peoples they sought to govern.[1] Therefore, in 1865, Malay was adopted as the second official language by the Dutch colonial government, who used it as an auxiliary language for local administration, commerce, and communication (Hoffman 1973).

Alisjahbana (1976) posits that ease of communication was not the only motivation of the Dutch for elevating Malay to official status, as demonstrated by their use of Malay as the primary medium of instruction for non-Europeans in the colonial school system. The Dutch did provide limited Dutch-language primary, secondary, and ultimately university instruction for the children of the Eurasian and Indonesian elites, but their general policy was to restrict the number of Indonesians who were proficient in Dutch, since Indonesians who completed their secondary and higher education in Dutch often competed with the Europeans for higher positions in government and commerce and for other privileges. Therefore, the Dutch established only 250 "Dutch Native" primary and secondary schools, with Dutch as the medium of instruction, for the Indonesian elites and a small group of intellectually promising non-elites (Alisjahbana 1976:114). The vast majority of Indonesians could attend only "Tweede Klasse" (Second Class) schools, in which the language of instruction was Malay (Nababan 1979:282; Central Bureau of Statistics 1940).

Actually, in pursuing this language policy, the Dutch contributed greatly to the modernization and standardization of Malay in Indonesia. Dutch administrators and scholars developed new registers for Malay in the many domains in which it was used; created a standardized Latin-alphabet spelling system for Malay, along with an extensive wordlist implementing this system; established a Malay-language publishing house to provide reading material on popular topics for Indonesians who had learned to read Malay in the schools; and supported a native journalistic press in Malay from the beginning of the current century (Alisjahbana 1976; Central Bureau of Statistics 1940; Nababan 1979).

However, the status of Malay was most greatly enhanced during the Dutch period through its role as a language of nationalism opposed to the colonial regime. Ironically, it was the Dutch language which equipped Malay for this function. Anderson (1966) observes that among the limited numbers of non-Europeans who received a Dutch-medium education, there developed a small group of intellectuals "without a real function within the structures of the colonial system," for whom proficiency in Dutch "opened the way to a critical conception of society as a whole, and a possible vision of a society after the disappearance of the colonial regime." Dutch "provided the necessary means of communication between the anti-imperialist and anti-colonial critiques of West European and, later, Russian Marxism and the potential revolutionary elite in Indonesia." From Dutch political tracts, "a socialist-communist vocabulary became the common property of the entire nationalist elite of those years" (Anderson 1966:101–102).

In seeking a single language through which to mobilize the Indonesian masses by means of these revolutionary ideas, the nationalists found Dutch unsatisfactory since so few people understood it. They likewise rejected Javanese, the most highly developed indigenous language, since it was associated with the largest and most powerful ethnic group and its use could therefore lead to dissension and mistrust from the non-Javanese. Moreover, as a reflection of the highly stratified Javanese social structure, most statements in the Javanese language require choices from a complicated hierarchy of morphosyntactic and lexical constructions, depending on the relative status of the interlocutors (Geertz 1960); Javanese was thus not at all suited for the expression of notions of equality and democracy central to revolutionary rhetoric.

In contrast to Dutch and Javanese, the nationalists found in Malay an indigenous language already widely used throughout the archipelago and ethnically neutral, in not being the first language of any prominent ethnic group. Moreover, Anderson (1966:104) has observed that as the primary trade language of the East Indies,

> it was a language simple and flexible enough to be rapidly developed into a modern political language . . . This was all the more possible because Malay as an 'inter-ethnic' language, or lingua franca, had *ipso facto* an almost statusless character, like Esperanto, and was tied to no particular regional social structure. It had thus a free, almost 'democratic' character from the outset. . . .

Thus, in the early decades of this century, the nationalists began actively promoting Malay as the best candidate for an Indonesian language, culminating in its adoption in October, 1928, at the second All-Indonesia Youth Congress in Surakarta, Central Java, as *Bahasa Indonesia*, "the Indonesian Language" (Alisjahbana 1976:39). In the 1930's, a genre of anti-colonial nationalist writing in Malay began to develop, spearheaded by a group of young Dutch-educated writers from Central and Northern Sumatra. Their variety of Malay, which was very similar to varieties of Malay spoken on the west coast of the Malay Peninsula, became the standard literary language for Indonesia and is still considered the standard model for education and formal occasions (Stevens 1973).

The Japanese occupation of Indonesia (1942–1945) further augmented the domains, functions, and status of Bahasa Indonesia. The Japanese abolished Dutch as the principal language of power of the Indies, hoping eventually to replace it with Japanese, which was taught as a compulsory subject in all the schools. However, the urgent wartime need to communicate quickly and clearly with the Indonesian people forced the Japanese to give Bahasa Indonesia official status in 1942 (Reid 1980) and to use it as the primary language of the islands. In their efforts to mobilize the Indonesians for the war effort, the Japanese went out to the most remote villiages, introducing Bahasa Indonesia in regions where it had never been used before (Alisjahbana 1976).

Furthermore, from early in their occupation, the Japanese

entertained the possibility of granting independence within their Greater East Asia Co-Prosperity Sphere to an Indonesian nation administered from Java. Later, as Japanese defeats began to augment, an independent Indonesia figured into their strategy of an insular defense perimeter around Japan (Elsbree 1953).

In pursuit of these objectives of immediate communication and preparation of a future ally, the Japanese contributed greatly to the further cultivation and elaboration of Bahasa Indonesia. They supported increases in the number and circulation of newspapers in Bahasa Indonesia, and provided public radio stands at parks, schools, and larger street intersections for Indonesians to hear lectures and speeches delivered in Bahasa Indonesia in support of the Japanese war effort (Elsbree 1953). In addition, the Japanese established Bahasa Indonesia as the primary language of government and law; science, technology, and industry; and of elementary through university education (Alisjahbana 1976).

This increased use and importance of Bahasa Indonesia required that it be standardized throughout the archipelago and that its lexicon be enlarged to function in new domains. To coordinate this linguistic retooling, the Japanese, beginning in 1942, established a series of language planning commissions with both Japanese and Indonesian members, whose task was to write a normative grammar, to standardize the existing vocabulary of daily usage, and to develop new terminology. By the end of the Japanese occupation, these commissions had added 7,000 new terms to the Indonesian language (Alisjahbana 1976; Reid 1980).

Concurrently, a small class of urban Indonesians—who during the Dutch colonial era had been treated as a privileged indigenous aristocracy, been educated in the Dutch-language schools, and subsequently used Dutch as their first language—were suddenly forbidden by the Japanese from speaking Dutch and therefore had to adopt Bahasa Indonesia as their primary language. This class, though not actively involved in the nationalist movement, had a high traditional status among the Indonesian population; their use of Bahasa Indonesia further expanded the domains of its use and added significantly to its prestige (Stevens 1973).

As a result of these myriad factors during the Dutch colonial period and the Japanese occupation, by the time the Japanese withdrew in defeat from Indonesia in August, 1945, the Malay language had undergone dramatic modernization and standardization, with sufficiently developed registers for government, law, education, science, and technology to function as the national language for a new nation. With virtually no opposition and no serious competition from any other language, endo- or exoglossic, Bahasa Indonesia was adopted as the sole national and official language of the new republic of Indonesia (Alisjahbana 1976).

Contemporary Indonesia

Under Indonesia's current language policy, adopted in 1976, Bahasa Indonesia remains the national and only official language. It is the symbol of identity and unity, the language of law and government administration, the primary medium of instruction in education, and a tool for national planning and for the development of science, technology, and national culture. In complementary distribution with Bahasa Indonesia, the regional languages are maintained for intra-regional communication and to preserve and develop local culture (Nababan 1979; 1982; Diah 1982).

In gaining popular acceptance of Bahasa Indonesia in these roles of national and official language, Indonesia is renowned for having experienced considerably more success than have most other newly independent multilingual nations. Factors most frequently cited as underlying this acceptance are identical to those responsible for Bahasa Indonesia's appeal during the colonial period: its central role as a vehicle and symbol of the movement for political independence, its ethnically neutral status in not being the first language of any prominent ethnic group, and the freedom it provides from encoding in all utterances distinctions in rank and status (Tanner 1967; Abas 1978; Harrison 1979; Nababan 1980; Diah 1982).

Concurrent with this general acceptance, proficiency in Bahasa Indonesia is becoming increasingly widespread among the Indonesian population. Reliable statistics are unavailable as to the numbers of Indonesians who could speak Bahasa Indonesia during the Dutch and Japanese colonial eras or even at the time of Indonesia's independence. However, recent census data indicate that general proficiency in Bahasa Indonesia is spreading very quickly. In the 1971 census, 40,250,000 Indonesians, or 40.7% of Indonesia's population, reported that they could speak Bahasa Indonesia. By 1980, this total had reached over 90,000,000, or 61% of the population (Nababan 1982; 1985).

The institution most often credited for this rapidly increasing proficiency in the national language is the educational system, particularly the compulsory six years of elementary school where the majority of Indonesians first learn and then use Bahasa Indonesia (Diah 1982; Douglas 1970; Tanner 1967). As stipulated in the national language policy, Bahasa Indonesia is the medium of instruction in all types of schools and at all levels of education throughout the country, with the exception that regional languages may be used as the medium of instruction during the first three years of primary school while Bahasa Indonesia is learned as a second language. Moreover, Bahasa Indonesia is also the major subject of instruction in the primary schools, being taught six to eight hours weekly for all six years, and is thereafter taught as a subject five hours per week during the three years of junior high school and at least three hours per week for the three years of senior high school (Aanenson 1979; Nababan 1982).

Besides providing access to proficiency in Bahasa Indonesia, the schools are also mandated by Indonesia's language policy to use the national language "as a means to strengthen and maintain the feeling of nationalism and unity." For example, the language arts curriculum in the secondary schools includes as writing models the nationalist literature in Bahasa Indonesia from the 1930's, mentioned earlier (Diah 1982:29).

In addition to the schools, Indonesia's education system is also increasing national proficiency in Bahasa Indonesia through an extensive non-formal education literacy program. Despite the fact that by 1980, 85% of all elementary school age children were enrolled in schools, due largely to financial considerations, only 50% of the pupils who entered the first grade were reaching the fourth grade, and only 35% were completing all six years (Beeby 1979; Diah 1982). For these Indonesians who do not attend school long enough to acquire literacy or proficiency in Bahasa Indonesia, the national Department of Education and Culture has since 1951 provided a series of "functional literacy" programs as part of its larger system of "non-formal education"—"organized learning opportunities outside the regular classroom" (Soedijarto et al. 1980:50). A primary goal in these programs has been proficiency and literacy in Bahasa Indonesia in order to write letters and to read newspapers, magazines, and other publications on a variety of practical topics (Lowenberg 1984; Napitupulu 1980).

A second major reason for the increasing use of Bahasa Indonesia has been urbanization. Since independence, increasing population pressure in rural regions has led to the tripling and quadrupling of the populations of Indonesia's cities, bringing together millions of Indonesians from different language backgrounds in new neighborhoods, at work, and in the marketplace (Peacock 1973). Attitudinally, the fact that Bahasa Indonesia is not the vernacular of any one prominent ethnic group has encouraged its acceptance for interethnic communication by urban Indonesians regardless of their first languages (Tanner 1967). An East Java study of fluency in Bahasa Indonesia in the late 1970's found that while fluency was still 30.8% in the villages, it had reached 60.8% in the urban areas (Harrison 1979). In addition, children of interethnic marriages, particularly in the urban centers, often acquire Bahasa Indonesia as their first language. Nababan (1985:3) reports that whereas at the time of Malay's adoption as Bahasa Indonesia, at most 500,000 Indonesians spoke it as a mother tongue, the 1980 census revealed over seventeen million Indonesians "who can legitimately be called 'native speakers' of Bahasa Indonesia."

The use of Bahasa Indonesia is also increasing in the domain of intraethnic communication among people sharing the same regional language as their mother tongue. Most of the regional languages of Indonesia, like Javanese mentioned above, require for any speech situation careful consideration of the relative status of the participants and observers (See, for example, Glicken 1982, for a description of the Sundanese language of West Java). In urban life, new social roles are created which may differ radically from traditional status relationships in the villages. As a result, participants in an urban speech act may stand in a superior-subordinate relationship in terms of a traditional hierarchy of ascribed status, such as nobility, but be social equals in terms of a newer hierarchy of achieved status, such as education and employment. Tanner (1967:24) notes that "in such ambiguous situations . . . individuals can avoid the difficulties and embarrassment involved in either proclaiming their equality or acknowledging their superiority or inferiority by communicating with one another in Indonesian" (ie. Bahasa Indonesia).

A third factor responsible for increasing proficiency in and use of Bahasa Indonesia has been the broadcast media. In accordance with the national language policy, all radio and television programming except that specifically promoting local culture is transmitted in Bahasa Indonesia from regional government stations to almost 2,000,000 radios and 20,000 television receivers throughout the country (Douglas 1970; *Europa Yearbook, 1982*; Vreeland et al. 1975).

As the foregoing discussion has demonstrated, Indonesia's often cited success in the selection, spread, and popular acceptance of her national language has resulted from a complex series of sociocultural, political, economic, and linguistic developments spanning more than a millenium. In Indonesia, Malay has evolved from a pre-colonial lingua franca, exhibiting considerable regional variation and functioning in a relatively restricted set of trade-related domains, into the primary shared code of over 160 million people,[2] with widespread status and prestige, a high degree of elaboration and cultivation adequate for use in virtually all linguistic domains of the modern world, a well-developed body of literature, and sufficient neutrality with regard to ethnicity and stylistic features to serve as one of the most popular national languages in the modern world.

Colonial Era: Malaya

The development and status of Malay in Malaysia and Singapore has been considerably different from that in Indonesia, due in large part to the policies of the British during their colonization of the Malay Peninsula and western Borneo (present-day Sabah, Sarawak, and Brunei) from the late eighteenth until the mid-twentieth centuries. Permanent British presence in the region effectively began with the establishment on the Malay Peninsula of the "Straits Settlements" of Penang (1796), Singapore (1819), and Malacca (1824) in order to support the British East India Company's tea trade with China. This initial period of British influence, in contrast to the highly restrictive immigration policy of the Dutch, noted above, was marked by large-scale immigration of Hokkien-speaking Chinese to the Straits Settlements, where they soon became the majority populations of Penang and Singapore (Platt, Weber, and Ho 1983). As will be seen, this concentration of Chinese in the coastal cities profoundly affected the future political, economic, and sociolinguistic development of the region.

In the 1870's, the British began to expand their influence more vigorously in the region until, by the end of the early twentieth century, they administered with varying degrees of direct control all of the Malay Peninsula and the crown colonies of Sarawak, Sabah, and Brunei on western Borneo (Vreeland et al. 1977a). Concurrent with this increasing British influence came further large-scale immigration to the region of Chinese and South Asians, the former to work in tin mines being opened in the interior of the Malay Peninsula, and the latter to develop rubber and coffee plantations and to construct a railroad (Hua 1983). Thus, by the time of its first census in 1911, the colony of Malaya had an extremely pluralistic society, including 1.5 million Malays, over 900,000 Chinese, and 267,000 Indians (Vreeland et al. 1977a). The predominant languages spoken by this diverse population included Malay; Hokkien, Teochew, Cantonese, Hakka, and Hainanese as the primary Chinese languages; and Tamil as the most widely used South Asian language, in addition to Malayalam, Telugu, and Punjabi (Platt and Weber 1980).

Another major difference between the British and the Dutch colonial policies was in the British provision of training in the principal colonial language of power, English, for large numbers of the non-European population. Actually the initial language policy of the British was very similar to that of the Dutch. Training in English and English-medium education was provided only to heirs of the royal and aristocratic Malay families to prepare them for employment as minor officials in the colonial civil service and the

Table 2 (Platt and Weber 1980:4)
Language and/or Dialect Divisions of the Main Ethnic Groups
at the Beginning of the Twentieth Century

Malays	Formal Malay
	Local Dialects according to region
	Native dialects of immigrants
Chinese	Hokkkien
	Teochew
	Cantonese
	Hakka
	Hainanese
	Others
Indians	*Southern Indian:*
	Mainly Tamil, Malayalam and Telugu
	Mainly Punjabi,
	Others

state governments (Vreeland et al. 1977a). Knowledge of English was not made available to the masses since, as argued by one of the British residents (in Platt and Weber 1980:6),

> I do not think it is advisable to attempt to give the children of an agricultural population an indifferent knowledge of a language that to all but the very few would only unfit them for the duties of life and make them discontent with anything like manual labour.

Furthermore, in accordance with a policy of "divide and rule," the British encouraged communal division of the non-Europeans along ethnic lines and did not wish to supply them with common proficiency, and thus potential power in colonial affairs, in English (Hassan 1975). Instead, the British used Malay, already well established as a lingua franca in the region, for some official purposes, requiring colonial officers to be proficient in Malay and, when necessary, employing interpreters, particularly Indians, who spoke both English and Malay (Alisjahbana 1976; Vreeland et al. 1977a).

However, as the volume of their mercantile trade expanded, in contrast to the more stable plantation economy of the Dutch, the British began to need a cadre of English-educated non-Europeans as an infrastructure of officials, business agents, and clerks. Hence, as early as the beginning of the nineteenth century, the colonial government established in the Straits Settlements and in other urban centers English-medium schools, where English was taught and then used as the medium of instruction and for other school activities. The students in these schools came from the more prosperous and prestigious families from all ethnic groups, especially the Chinese and Indians, whose parents wanted them prepared for entry into government service, positions in trade and commerce, and the professions (Platt, Weber, and Ho 1983). Malay-medium schools were also established; however, due to insufficient resources and trained personnel, instruction was greatly inferior to that in the English-medium schools (Alisjahbana 1976). Most secondary schools were conducted in English, as was instruction at Raffles College and at the Singapore Medical College (Platt and Weber 1980; Vreeland et al. 1977a).

Largely as a result of these English-medium schools, the use of English continually increased during the colonial era, almost totally replacing Malay at all levels and in most domains of government, including administration and the legal system, domestic and international commerce, and transportation and communication (Platt and Weber 1980).

More significant for the status of Malay in contemporary Malaysia and Singapore, English also became the language of power and prestige among the urban non-European elites throughout the colony, particularly as the primary code for interethnic communication among the Chinese, Indian, and Malay elites who attended the English-medium schools and then continued to use English in a wide variety of domains as adults (Platt and Weber 1980; Vreeland et al. 1977a). By the end of the colonial era, English had become "a lingua franca among the more educated sections of the community" (Le Page 1962:133).

A final factor leading to the lesser status of Malay in colonial Malaya than in colonial Indonesia was the Japanese occupation. As in Indonesia, the Japanese initially attempted to promote the

Japanese language among the occupied population, only to discover that the population could not learn the Japanese language quickly enough to sustain the war effort. However, whereas Malay had been sufficiently developed under the Dutch to be adopted by the Japanese as an official language in Indonesia, the emphasis on English in British Malaya had left Malay linguistically unequipped for use in modern domains. Hence, the Japanese were forced to reinstate limited use of English, which they had originally prohibited, or else "the administrative structure of Malaya, which they had so hastily set up, would simply collapse like a deck of cards" (Chin 1946:156; Cheah 1983).

In addition, while the Japanese supported the development of Bahasa Indonesia as a step toward Indonesian independence, they never seriously considered independence for Malaya, most of which they considered economically and politically backward. Instead, the Japanese intended to rule the Straits Settlements directly, with the remainder of Malaya administered from Singapore as a protectorate (Akashi 1980; Elsbree 1953).

Thus perceiving no possibility of using Malay for communication or need to develop it as the official language for a future independent ally—their motives for supporting Bahasa Indonesia—the Japanese put little effort into the promotion of Malay in Malaya. By the end of the Japanese occupation, in contrast to the numerous functional domains for which Bahasa Indonesia had been modernized and standardized, the functions of Malay in the former British territories were still extremely restricted.

Post-Colonial Malaya

Nevertheless, in 1957, at the time of its independence from the British (who had regained colonial control after World War II), the *Federation of Malaya*, consisting of the Malay Peninsula except for Singapore, adopted not English but Malay as its sole national language. Ostensibly, this selection resulted from two considerations: (1) a desire to have an endoglossic language, for which Malay was the most widely used candidate, as a symbol of and vehicle for national identity and integration; and (2) the fact that when the British withdrew, only the 10% of the population who had comprised the non-European elites during the colonial era could speak English (Hassan 1975; Le Page 1962). However, an equally important and explicitly formulated goal was to accord favored status to the Malays, the largest and therefore potentially the most politically powerful ethnic group, in their economic competition with the descendants of the Chinese and Indian immigrants. These non-Malays—especially the Chinese by virtue of their concentrations in the urban coastal centers,[3] where they had long been using English—had during the colonial period gained a significant economic advantage over the Malays (Le Page 1962; Vreeland et al. 1977a).

Nonetheless, the formulators of this language policy also recognized the continued importance of English as the only language in post-World War II Malaya that was linguistically equipped for the myriad functions of a modern nation. Hence, a policy was devised for both Malay and English to have official status until 1967, a ten-year transition period during which Malay was to be taught intensively and modernized so that it could serve as the sole official language and medium of instruction in the schools (Platt and Weber 1980; Vreeland et al. 1977a). Two government agencies were established to help achieve this goal—a Language Institute, to train educators from all ethnic groups to teach in Malay, and the *Dewan Bahasa dan Pustaka* (the "Language and Literature Agency") to prepare Malay-language textbooks and teaching materials, produce a standardized Malay dictionary, coin and adopt new words for the lexical modernization of Malay, and promote the use of Malay among the general population (Le Page 1962).

However, beyond establising these agencies, the government took few firm steps to implement this goal, relying instead on "persuasion" to have Malay replace English over the allotted ten years (Hassan 1975:3). As a result, there occurred a "linguistic drift toward English," which provided "the main avenues to higher education and economic advancement" (Le Page 1962:142). Prestigious scholarships to universities and training institutes in the British Commonwealth and in the United States were available exclusively to candidates with a high proficiency in English. Similarly, only those who could functionally use English were eligible for the best employment, both within and outside Government service (Le Page 1964).

Not surprisingly, the majority of Malayan students continued to be enrolled in English-medium schools. In fact, the percentage of the total enrollment from all ethnic groups in government subsidized secondary schools who chose English as the medium of instruction increased from 61.0% in 1956 to 84.4% in 1964 (Platt and Weber 1980). Even among the ethnic Malays, Le Page observed in the early 1960's (1962:141)

> fairly keen competition, among those Malay parents who are ambitious for their children, to get them into English-medium schools, and indeed the Malay elite are still educated at schools such as Malay College where the teaching is wholly in English.

Contemporary Malaysia

What ultimately catalyzed more vigorous implementation of the language policy was a dramatic rise in ethnic communalism that developed in the region during the 1960's. A major source of tension, discussed in detail below, was Singapore's political unification with the Federation of Malaya, Sabah, and Sarawak in an expanded nation of Malaysia, followed only two years later by Singapore's secession from the new polity. In addition, developments on the Malay Peninsula—including an economy greatly weakened by declining rubber prices and discontent among the Malay elites at the slow pace with which their economic condition was improving relative to that of the Chinese Malaysians—further threatened the stability of the ethnic concord essential to Malaysia's survival, culminating in serious Malay-Chinese riots in the late 1960's (Hua 1983; Vreeland et al. 1977b).

In an effort to appease the Malay plurality in the population[4] and to diffuse ethnic tensions by promoting Malaysian identity, the Malaysian government in the second half of the 1960's began to take more determined steps to strengthen the position of Malay, which it renamed a more ethnically neutral *Bahasa Malaysia* (literally, the "Malaysian Language"). In 1967, a revised National Language Act specified Bahasa Malaysia as the only language for most official documents and publications, and as the primary

Table 3 (based on Encyclopedia Britannica 1984:514)
Percentage of Main Ethnic Groups in Malaysia, 1980 (estimated)
(Total Population 14,995,000) (1983 estimate)

Malay	47.1%
Chinese	32.7%
Indian	9.6%
Other	10.6%

language for use in Parliament and the courts; furthermore, it required passing a proficiency test in Bahasa Malaysia for promotion in government service. In 1969, the Ministry of Education initiated a policy whereby all English-medium schools changed to Malay-medium in the first year of primary school; thereafter, on a year-by-year basis English-medium was replaced by Malay-medium instruction until by 1983, virtually all primary and secondary education nationwide was conducted in Bahasa Malaysia. In 1970, Universiti Kebangsaan became the first totally Malay-medium tertiary institution. At present, in other universities, Bahasa Malaysia is being used increasingly in lectures and course examinations, and all candidates for admission to government-supported higher education are now required to pass entrance tests in Bahasa Malaysia (Hua 1983; Llamzon 1978; Platt and Weber 1980).

Advocates of this language policy claim that it has met with considerable success, pointing out that Bahasa Malaysia is now spoken by over 80% of the population, whereas only 44% were proficient in it in 1970 (Llamzon 1978). In addition, they observe, Bahasa Malaysia is being used increasingly via code-mixing and code-switching in intraethnic communication among Chinese and Indian Malaysians (Asmah 1982).

However, among these significant portions of the Malaysian population who are not ethnically Malays, there appears to be less than wholehearted acceptance of the national language. Llamzon (1978:90) observes that

> the feeling is prevalant, though frequently unexpressed, that the language is still very much identified with a group; that Bahasa Malaysia

is unable to transcend the narrow confines of its ethnic identity; that the propagation of the language is nothing more than an attempt on the part of its native speakers to assert their superiority and heighten rivalry and competition by placing the other groups in the country at a disadvantage.

For example, Sabah and Sarawak, the provinces of East Malaysia on the island of Borneo, which joined Malaysia with Singapore in 1963, have both been hesitant to switch totally from English to Bahasa Malaysia, a reluctance at least partially due to a fear of Malay domination over their largely non-Malay populations (Le Page 1962; Vreeland et al. 1977a).

In addition, there is evidence that this language policy may not even be beneficial to the majority of the ethnic Malays. The emerging standard variety of Bahasa Malaysia, used in the national government, the mass media, and textbooks in the schools, is basically that of the ethnic Malay elites living in the capital, Kuala Lumpur, and the other population center of southern Malaysia, Jahore Bahru (Le Page 1985). In contrast, close to 90% of the Malays live in rural areas and speak such regional varieties of Malay as Kedah Malay, Kelantan Malay, and Sarawak Malay, many of which differ radically in their linguistic features from the standard (Rogers 1982).

These differences are augmented by considerable transfer of features at all linguistic levels, from morphology and syntax to discourse and style, which have entered standard Bahasa Malaysia through contact with Chinese, Tamil, Bahasa Indonesia, and especially English via the usage of the urban Malay elites (Asmah 1982; Le Page 1985). A combination of interference from non-standard varieties of Malay, inadequately trained teachers, and a dearth of teaching materials in the rural schools has resulted in rural Malay students generally experiencing more difficulty in mastering standard Bahasa Malaysia than do the urban non-Malay native speakers of other languages "who study Bahasa Malaysia as an object in the classroom" (Le Page 1985:35). In addition, contrary to the non-formal education programs, discussed earlier, which are bringing both literacy and proficiency in Bahasa Indonesia to the rural population of Indonesia, de Terra (1983:536) claims that no such literacy campaigns are being pursued in Malaysia, and that "Bahasa Malaysia is not available to all."

This situation has caused some observers to question the basic intent of Malaysia's national language policy. For example, de Terre (1983:531) concludes that the selection and cultivation of Bahasa Malaysia as the sole national and official language has resulted largely from the pursuit of class interests by the urban Malay elites rather than a means to achieve ethnic equality and promote national unity and integration:

> the language chosen to erase the identification of one ethnic group (the Chinese) with economic and/or academic advantage is the language of another ethnic group (the Malays). Within that other ethnic group, it is the language of one class that makes use of ethnicity to further its own class interests. [my parentheses]

The test of this conclusion regarding the role of Bahasa Malaysia as a national language will be the degree and speed with which the rural Malays and other ethnic minorities can gain access to literacy and proficiency in the prestige variety of Bahasa Malaysia and thereby begin to share in the economic benefits of Malaysia's development.

Singapore

The selection and retention of Malay as the national language of Singapore has been less controversial than in Malaysia and less consequential than in either Malaysia or Indonesia. Whereas the status of Malay in Malaysia and Indonesia has resulted from a number of *intra*national factors, Singapore's selection of Malay was originally and still is motivated by largely *inter*national socioeconomic and political concerns.

Singapore was first granted a degree of self-government in 1959; however, out of concern for their economic and political security following the eventual complete withdrawal of the British, Singapore's leaders had begun proposing unification with the Federation of Malaya as early as 1957, the year in which the Federation became independent. Malaya was initially reluctant to merge with Singapore due to the latter's Chinese population at the time of 1.1 million, a legacy of the previously discussed immigration patterns of the Chinese during the colonial era. These Singaporean

Table 4 (based on Encyclopedia Britannica 1984:612)
Percentage of Main Ethnic Groups in Singapore, 1982
(estimated)
(Total Population 2,502,000) (1983 estimate)

Chinese	76.7%
Malay	14.7%
Indian	6.4%
Other	2.2%

Chinese, if added to Malaya's 2.3 million Chinese, would cause a new, combined state to have a larger Chinese than Malay population (Vreeland et al. 1977b).

In order to convince Malaya that unification would not present a threat to the Federation's already fragile interethnic stability, Singapore in 1959 adopted Malay as its single national language and the primary medium of instruction in its schools. That this policy was motivated by the desire for unification with Malaya is indicated by an official language policy statement at the time which argued that granting this status to Malay "will help us to cross the Straits of Johore [separating Malaya and Singapore] into the Federation" (cited in Gopinathan 1974:34).

This policy was by no means empty rhetoric. For the next five years, Singapore did more than Malaya to promote the status of Malay, including (Gopinathan 1974)

> the provision of a subsidy to the Adult Education Board to conduct Malay language classes, the making of the study of the national language compulsory in the schools, (and) the requirement that confirmation in posts of the Civil Service was dependent on civil servants passing the government's national language examination (p. 40) . . . Special courses were run to meet the demand this made on teachers, and in order to encourage the development of the language itself the government established the National Language and Culture Institute (p. 34).

A year earlier, an official "special policy" had already been adopted toward the Malays, "motivated both by a desire to alleviate backwardness and to improve by a pro-Malay policy the chances of merger of Singapore with Malaya" (Gopinathan 1974:40). This policy was made explicit in a 1958 "Constitution-Order in Council" that it would be "the deliberate and conscious policy of government to recognize the special position of the Malays, who are the indigenous people of the island and most in need of assistance" (cited in Buss 1958:54). Toward this end, Malay students were offered free primary, secondary, and university education; additional scholarships and other financial support; free textbooks; and special transportation allowances (Gopinathan 1974).

These policies regarding the Malay language and its native speakers appear to have enhanced Malaya's confidence that political merger with Singapore could succeed. In addition, concern over a strong left-wing political movement in Singapore that had been steadily growing since the mid-1950's further motivated the Malayans to unite with Singapore in order to avoid ultimately having a Communist Chinese city-state as a neighbor. Therefore, in September, 1963, as noted above, the expanded nation of Malaysia was formed by a merger of the Federation of Malaya, Singapore, and the crown colonies of Sabah and Sarawak, the latter being included in part for their largely non-Chinese populations, which ensured that the majority of the Malaysian population would still be peoples indigenous to the region (Vreeland et al. 1977a).

However, Singapore's participation in this union was short-lived for a number of political reasons. One major ideological difference between the former Federation and Singapore stemmed from the latter's refusal to formulate a plan to make Malay its *sole* official language, which, as discussed earlier, the Federation had already done at its inception. A critical domain of this policy division was the educational system, in which Singapore declared no intention of converting to a system of all Malay-medium schools from its four "streams" of schools, each with a different primary language of instruction—English as the colonial legacy, and Malay, Mandarin, and Tamil as options for the major ethnic groups (Gopinathan 1974). Another source of conflict was dissatisfaction among a large sector of Singapore's population concerning their deliberate under-representation in the lower house of the Malaysian Parliament, a condition which the Federation of Malaya had demanded in order to maintain the delicate balance of power between Malays and Chinese. These differences quickly exacerbated tensions throughout the Malay Peninsula, leading to ethnic riots in Singapore in 1964, and culminating in Singapore's withdrawal from Malaysia as an independent nation in August, 1965 (Gopinathan 1974; Vreeland et al. 1977b).

Despite these interethnic conflicts, at the time of its secession from Malaysia, Singapore's leaders elected to retain Malay as the sole national language. In so doing, their motives, as in their original adoption of Malay, were again largely international, particularly to promote cooperation and good will with Singapore's Malay-speaking neighbors, Indonesia and Malaysia. Had *intra*national concerns been of primary importance, other languages would have been more logical candidates. Given an over 75% Chinese population[5] speaking a large range of Chinese languages, Mandarin as a neutral, pan-Chinese tongue would have been one possible choice. However, the continued presence in Singapore of highly vocal left-wing political parties was already a matter of considerable concern among the vehemently anti-communist governments of Indonesia and Malaysia, a distrust which might have been aggravated by giving national status to the dominant language of the People's Republic of China. Another possibility for the national language was English as the predominant interethnic link language of Singapore's colonial period. However, selection of English could likewise have been construed by Singapore's neighbors as reflecting identity of interests with foreign powers. Thus, largely as an expression of solidarity with Indonesia and Malaysia—with whom Singapore has subsequently entered the Association of Southeast Asian Nations (ASEAN), as well as joined forces in several bi- and trilateral projects—Singapore has maintained Malay as its sole national language (Kuo 1977).

Nevertheless, since independence, the status that Singapore has accorded to Malay has never approximated either its degree of intentional association with the ethnic Malays or its functional significance prior to Singapore's joining and seceding from Malaysia. National policies have consistently been formulated without particular attention to the interests of the ethnic Malays (Gopinathan 1974; Vreeland et al. 1977b). Similarly, the domains reserved solely for Malay as the national language have been greatly diminished to largely ceremonial functions: the national coat of arms, the National Anthem, military commands, and protocol rituals at official functions (Kuo 1977; Llamzon 1978). In all other domains controlled in any way by the government, including the education system, Malay shares status as an official language with Mandarin, Tamil, and English. The intent of this multilingual policy, as it already was in the school system before independence, has been to promote the three non-European languages in order to maintain ethnic identity and cultural diversity, while using English in the domains of administration and law, in interethnic communication, and in international commerce in the world's fourth busiest seaport (Vreeland et al. 1977b).

Since the promulgation of this policy, the most noteworthy development in language status in Singapore has been not this diminished importance of Malay, but a largely unforeseen increase in the use of English. Initially intended to function in a largely auxiliary capacity, English is rapidly becoming the most widely used language in several linguistic domains. In the domain of employment, much intra-governmental communication and correspondence is conducted in English (Platt and Weber 1980); English is the only language used in interviews for government positions and is crucial for advancements in employment with the Singapore civil service (Tay 1982). In the private sector, both large and small businesses are increasingly using English as one or the only language of intra-office communication, particularly at management levels (Platt and Weber 1980). With the exception of some Chinese firms, job interviews are conducted in English, and once hired, employees' competence in English is an important criterion in their promotion (Tay 1982). In addition, English-educated employees consistently earn higher monthly incomes than do employees of the same age and level of education who have been educated in other languages of instruction (Kuo 1977).

In the Singapore school system, Malay, Mandarin, Tamil, and English continue to share equal status as official languages of instruction, in that parents can choose to send their children to

Chinese-, Malay-, Tamil-, or English-medium primary and secondary schools. However, owing to the importance of English in the domain of employment, the percentage of primary and secondary students, from all ethnic groups, enrolled in English-medium schools increased consistently from 31.6% in 1947 to 71.3% in 1976 (Platt and Weber 1980). This trend has accelerated since developments in 1975 made university education in Singapore available only in English; by 1980, 84.5% of elementary school pupils were being taught in English (Le Page 1984).

This increasing enrollment in English-medium schools has occurred despite frequent pleas by government leaders for parents to enroll their children in other language medium schools, appeals motivated by a concern that Singapore's rich linguistic and cultural heritage may be erased by the dominance of English. However, as Singapore's bilingual education policy allows all children to use the mother tongue of their ethnic background as a second medium of instruction for selected subjects, Kuo (1977:22) observes that the option of sending their children to English-medium schools "becomes easier for the parents because they can now send their children to English schools for economic advancement without any guilty feeling of betraying their ethnic tradition."

A related consequence of this increasing use of English in the schools and on the job has been a rise in the use of English in informal conversation. During the colonial era, as discussed above, English had already become an important code for interethnic communication, especially among the educated sector of the population. A more dramatic development since Singapore's independence has been the widespread use of English for *intra*ethnic conversation among all ethnic groups. In these cases, English is often mixed and switched with other languages when speakers wish to signal their status, education, or a change in register (cf. Lowenberg 1985; Platt and Weber 1980; Richards 1982).

The increasing use of English in Singapore is also reflected in other domains, including rising circulations in English-language newspapers and magazines and growing percentages of English-language programming and advertising on radio and television (Platt and Weber 1980). These trends, together with the patterns of English use just described, have led some observers, such as Llamzon (1978:92), to argue that English is rapidly becoming not only the most widely used of Singapore's official languages, but also the replacement of Malay as Singapore's *de facto* national language.

Nevertheless, a great many Singaporeans continue to be proficient in and use Malay. Kuo (1980) reports statistics that among all Singaporeans who were fifteen years or older in 1978, Malay was the major Singapore language in which the largest percentage (67.3) claimed to be competent, followed by Mandarin (63.9%) and English (61.7%). This higher competence in Malay than in the other official languages was found to occur among Malays, South Asians, and Chinese.

Of the individual ethnic groups, 99.8% of the Malays claimed competence in Malay—the highest mother-tongue retention rate in Singapore (Kuo 1978a). Subsequent data from the 1980 census indicated that 97.7% of all Malays five years of age or older used Malay as the principal language of the home (Tay 1985a). These high rates of retention and use of Malay by the Malays have been attributed to their being Singapore's most homogeneous group, both linguistically and ethnically (Tay 1985a), and to their indigeneous status in the region, making them the "host culture" and less likely to assimilate with the groups whose ancestors immigrated during the colonial era (Kuo 1978a:87).

Malay is also frequently used by many Singaporeans of South Asian descent, of whom 97.4% claimed competence in Malay in 1978 (Kuo 1980). Within this group, the 1980 census indicated that 9.3% use Malay as the primary language of the home (Anderson 1985), a percentage which may be considerably higher among the 36% of the South Asians whose mother tongue is not Tamil.

With regard to the future, recent studies predict the continued use of Malay in Singapore. Data from the 1980 census indicate retention of Malay by the Malays and by those South Asians for whom it is the principal language of the home. Anderson (1985:93) finds "a very strong pattern of maintenance" across the current three generations living in most Malay families. In fact, Tay (1985a) reports much higher use of Malay as the primary language of the household among younger (ages 5 to 24 years) than older (over 24 years) Singaporeans, and a tendency (81.9%) to listen to

Malay-language radio programs among Singaporeans for whom Malay is the primary home language. She concludes (Tay 1985a:16) that

> of all the languages and dialects in Singapore, Malay appears to be the one language that will continue to be used as the principal home language by those who (currently) use it . . . It is unlikely to be superseded by another language, such as English. [my parentheses].

Another factor that Tay (1985b) suggests may contribute to the continued acquisition and use of Malay by Singaporeans is the increasing employment, as Singapore's standard of living improves, of Malay and Indonesian women as caretakers in child-care centers and as live-in "amahs" (baby-sitters) or maids in Singapore households of all ethnic groups. Tay posits (1985b:8) that the caretaker language spoken by these women "will influence a person's use of language in childhood much more than the traditionally defined mother tongue."

Beyond the domain of the home, a study by Lim (1980:26) revealed that in Singapore's bilingual education policy, in which, as noted earlier, students select their second language of instruction, "Malay is the most popular second language in that there were Chinese, Indians, and other races learning it rather than their own native language in school."

Evidently, the language situation in Singapore is still very much in flux. Although the over-all dominance of English in employment and education appears likely to continue in the foreseeable future, there are several indications that Malay is far from dying, and will likewise continue to retain considerable status in a number of domains.

Conclusion

Undoubtedly, Malay's long use as the dominant lingua franca throughout present-day Indonesia, Malaysia, and Singapore is at least partly responsible for its current status as the national language of all three of these countries. But equally significant have been political and economic developments during and subsequent to the colonial era, developments that have created sociolinguistic contexts in which the motives for and the results of Malay's obtaining this status have diverged considerably. In Indonesia, the acceptance and use of Bahasa Indonesia as an ethnically neutral symbol of national identity and integration has been so successful as to be the envy of the multilingual world. Credit for this development, however, belongs not only to the wisdom of the Indonesian nationalists who first promoted Malay for this role, but also to the language policies of the Dutch and Japanese, who, motivated by practical concerns of self-interest, encouraged the use of Bahasa Indonesia and contributed crucially in equipping it to serve as an official language in support of its national status.

In Malaysia, the selection and promotion of Bahasa Malaysia as the national language has been motivated at least in part by ethnic communalism rather than national unity, a situation which has greatly impeded its acceptance as the national language. Yet Malaysia's difficulties can likewise be attributed at least partially to the immigration and language policies of the British and the Japanese, particularly the former, which have left Malaysia with two ethnic populations of almost the same size and no neutral language as a viable option for compromise.

In largely Chinese Singapore, Malay as a national language appears to have little connection with *intra*national identity, but rather serves to express Singapore's *inter*national integration and unity with her two closest neighbors. The noteworthy development in Singapore, of course, is the continually increasing domination of English, once again a legacy provided, especially to the Chinese, by the British colonial policies. Concurrently, the comfortable demographic superiority that the Chinese enjoy, which likewise results from British immigration policies, protects Malay from being perceived as the vested interest of an ethnic rival, with the result that Malay continues to flourish in interpersonal domains.

Meanwhile, the status of and domains served by the languages of these three multilingual countries are far from static. In Indonesia, Malay was originally selected in part to offset the traditional dominance of the Javanese. However, since independence, as positions of power have tended to be occupied by the Javanese,

Bahasa Indonesia has been altered by substantial transfer from Javanese at all linguistic levels, occasionally provoking concern among other ethnic groups that the neutrality of the national language is being eroded (Abas 1978; Stevens 1973). Concurrently, Malaysia has found that its long dependence on English, both domestically and internationally, cannot be eradicated as easily as had been hoped in the late 1960's, and a concerted push to upgrade English in recent years (Le Page 1984; Rogers 1982) may dilute the linguistic hegemony that Bahasa Malaysia has enjoyed for the past decade. In Singapore, the government for several years has been attempting to promote the use of Mandarin among the Chinese, partly in an effort to balance the dominance of English (Le Page 1984). To the degree that this campaign is effective, official interest in Malay may revive as well. Kuo (1978b) reports that the Singapore government has been considering participation in on-going joint Malaysian-Indonesian language planning activities toward the standardization and modernization of Bahasa Indonesia and Bahasa Malaysia.

In sum, as elsewhere in the world, the contexts of language use in the Malay Archipelago are constantly evolving and changing. As they do, the status and functions of Malay in the region will likewise continue to shift with other linguistic and non-linguistic developments and thereby shed further light on the many complexities of the national language question.

References

Aanenson, C. R. 1979. *Indonesia*. Washington, DC: American Association of College Registrars and Admissions Officers.

Abas, Husen. 1978. Bahasa Indonesia as a unifying language of wider communication: a historical and sociolinguistic perspective. Unpublished doctoral dissertation, Ateneo de Manila University-Philippine Normal College Consortium, Manila.

Akashi, Yoji. 1980. The Japanese occupation of Malaya: interruption or transformation? In McCoy ed., 65–89.

Alisjahbana, S. Takdir. 1976. *Language planning and modernization: the case of Indonesian and Malaysian*. The Hague: Mouton.

Anderson, Benedict R. 1966. The languages of Indonesian politics. *Indonesia* 1(1): 89–106.

Anderson, Edmund A. 1985. Sociolinguistic surveys in Singapore. *International Journal of the Sociology of Language* 55: 89–114.

Asmah, Haji Omar. 1982. Language spread and recession in Malaysia and the Malay Archipelago. In Robert L. Cooper ed., *Language Spread: studies in diffusion and social change*. Bloomington: Indiana University Press, 198–213.

Beeby, C. E. 1979. *Assessment of Indonesian education: a guide in planning.* Wellington, New Zealand: Oxford University Press.

Britannica Book of the Year, 1986. Chicago: Encyclopedia Britannica, Inc.

Buss, Claude. 1958. *Southeast Asia and the world today.* Princeton: D. Van Nostrand.

Cady, John F. 1964. *Southeast Asia: its historical development.* New York: McGraw Hill.

Central Bureau of Statistics, Department of Economic Affairs. 1940. *Pocket edition of the statistical abstract of the Netherlands Indies, 1940.* Batavia: Netherlands Information Bureau.

Cheah Boon Kheng. 1983. *Red star over Malaya: resistance and social conflict during and after the Japanese occupation of Malaya, 1941–46.* Singapore: University of Singapore Press.

Chin Kee Onn. 1946. *Malaya upside down.* Singapore: Jitts and Company.

de Terra, Diane. 1983. The linguagenesis of society: the implementation of the national language plan in West Malaysia. In Bruce Bain ed., *The sociogenesis of language and human contact.* New York: Plenum Press, 527–540.

Diah, M. 1982. *National language policy and the writing curriculum in Indonesia: a case study.* Urbana: Curriculum Laboratory, University of Illinois.

Douglas, Stephen A. 1970. *Political socialization and student activism in Indonesia.* Urbana: University of Illinois Press.

Dyen, Isadore. 1971. The Austronesian languages and Proto-Austronesian. In Thomas A. Sebeok ed., *Current trends in linguistics.* Vol. 8, Part 1. The Hague: Mouton, 5–54.

Elsbree, Willard H. 1953. *Japan's role in Southeast Asian nationalist movements, 1940 to 1945.* Cambridge, MA: Harvard University Press.

Europa yearbook, 1982. Vol. 2. London: Europa Publications, Ltd.

Geertz, Clifford. 1960. *The religion of Java.* Glencoe, IL: The Free Press.

Glicken, Jessica. 1982. Sundanese Islam and the value of hormat: control, obedience, and social location in West Java. Paper presented at Indonesian Summer Studies Institute Conference, 12–15 August, 1982, Athens, Ohio.

Gonda, J. 1973. *Sanskrit in Indonesia.* New Delhi: International Academy of Indian Culture.

Gopinathan, Saravanan. 1974. *Towards a national system of education in Singapore, 1945–1973.* Singapore: Oxford University Press.

Harrison, Brian. 1967. *South-east Asia: a short history* (third edition). New York: St. Martin's Press.

Harrison, Selig S. 1979. Why they won't speak our language in Asia. *Asia* 1(6): 3–7.

Hassan, Abdullah. 1975. The standardization and promotion of Bahasa Malaysia. Paper given at Regional English Language Centre Conference, January, 1975, Bangkok, Thailand.

Hoffman, J. E. 1973. The Malay Language as a force for unity in the Indonesian Archipelago, 1815–1900. *Nusantara*, No. 4, 19–36.

Hua Wu Yin. 1983. *Class and communalism in Malaysia*. London: Marram Books.

Kuo, Eddie C. Y. 1977. The status of English in Singapore: a sociolinguistic analysis. In William Crewe ed., *The English Language in Singapore*. Singapore: Eastern Universities Press, 10–33.

Kuo, Eddie C. Y. 1978a. Population ratio, intermarriage and mother tongue retention. *Anthropological Linguistics* 20(2): 85–93.

Kuo, Eddie C. Y. 1978b. Language planning in Singapore. *Language Planning Newsletter* 6(2): 1–5.

Kuo, Eddie C. Y. 1980. The sociolinguistic situation in Singapore: unity in diversity. In E. A. Afendras and Eddie C. Y. Kuo eds. *Language and society in Singapore*. Singapore: University of Singapore Press, 39–62.

Le Page, Robert B. 1962. Multilingualism in Malaya. In *Symposium on multilingualism* [second meeting of the Inter-African Committee on Linguistics, 16–21 July, 1962, Brazzaville]. London: Committee for Technical Cooperation in Africa.

Le Page, Robert B. 1984. Retrospect and prognosis in Malaysia and Singapore. *International Journal of the Sociology of Language* 45: 113–126.

Le Page, Robert B. 1985. The language standardisation problems of Malaysia set in context. *Southeast Asian Journal of Social Science* 13(1): 29–39.

Lim Kiat Boey. 1980. Language learning and language use among some Singapore students. *RELC Journal* 11(2): 10–28

Llamzon, Teodoro A. 1978. English and the national languages in Malaysia, Singapore and the Philippines: a sociolinguistic comparison. *Cross Currents* 5(1): 87–104.

Lowenberg, Peter H. 1984. Literacy in Indonesia. In Robert B. Kaplan ed., *Annual Review of Applied Linguistics, 1983*, 124–140. Rowley, MA: Newbury House.

Lowenberg, Peter H. 1985. Nativization and function in ESL: A case study. *TESL Studies* 6: 88–107.

McCoy, Alfred W. ed. 1980. *Southeast Asia under Japanese occupation*. New Haven: Yale University Southeast Asia Studies. [Monograph Series no. 22]

Nababan, P. W. J. 1979. Languages of Indonesia. In Teodoro A. Llamzon ed., *Papers on Southeast Asian languages*. Singapore: SEAMEO Regional Language Centre, 259–291.

Nababan, P. W. J. 1980. Proficiency profiles: a study in bilingualism and bilinguality in Indonesia. In Lim Kiat Boey ed., *Bilingual education*. Singapore: SEAMEO Regional Language Centre, 209–221.

Nababan, P. W. J. 1982. Indonesia. In Noss ed., 1–47.

Nababan, P. W. J. 1985. Bilingualism in Indonesia: ethnic language maintenance and the spread of the national language. *Southeast Asian Journal of Social Science* 13(1): 1–18.

Napitupulu, W. P. 1980. Illiteracy eradication programme in Indonesia (The Learning Package A Kejar Programme). Paper presented at workshop on Planning and Administration of National Literacy Programmes, Arusha, Tanzania, 27 November–2 December.

Noss, Richard B. ed. 1982. *Language teaching issues in multilingual environments in Southeast Asia*. Singapore: SEAMEO Regional Language Centre. [RELC Anthology Series no. 10]

Peacock, James L. 1973. *Indonesia: an anthropological perspective*. Pacific Palisades, CA: Goodyear Publishing Company.

Platt, John and Heidi Weber. 1980. *English in Singapore and Malaysia*. New York: Oxford University Press.

Platt, John, Heidi Weber, and Mian Lian Ho. 1983. *Singapore and Malaysia*. Amsterdam and Philadelphia: John Benjamins. [Vol. 4 in series Varieties of English around the World]

Reid, Anthony. 1980. Indonesia: from briefcase to samurai sword. In McCoy ed., 17–32.

Richards, Jack C. 1982. Singapore English: rhetorical and communicative styles. In Braj B. Kachru ed., *The other tongue*. Urbana: University of Illinois Press, 154–167.

Rogers, Anthony J. 1982. Malaysia. In Noss ed., 48–77.

Soedijarto et al. 1980. Indonesia. In T. N. Postlethwaite and R. M. Thomas eds., *Schooling in the ASEAN region*. Oxford: Pergamon Press, 48–96.

Stevens, Alan M. 1973. Bahasa Indonesia: modernization and nationalization. *Asia* (1973), 70–84.

Tanner, Nancy. 1967. Speech and society among the Indonesian elite, a case study of a multilingual community. *Anthropological Linguistics* 9(3): 15–40.

Tay, Mary W. J. 1982. The uses, users, and features of English in Singapore. In John Pride ed., *New Englishes*. Rowley, MA: Newbury House, 51–70.

Tay, Mary W. J. 1985a. *Trends in language, literacy and education in Singapore*. Singapore: Department of Statistics. [Census Monograph no. 2]

Tay, Mary W. J. 1985b. Patterns of bilingualism in Singapore: language, function, and use. Manuscript. Department of English, University of Singapore.

Teeuw, A. 1967. *Modern Indonesian literature*. The Hague: Martinus Nijhoff.

Voegelin, C. F. and F. M. Voegelin. 1964. Languages of the world: Indo-Pacific fascicle four. *Anthropological Linguistics* 7(2): 2–297.

Vreeland, Nena et al. 1975. *Area handbook for Indonesia* (third edition). Washington, DC: The American University.

Vreeland, Nena et al. 1977a. *Area handbook for Malaysia* (third edition). Washington, DC: The American University.

Vreeland, Nena et al. 1977b. *Area handbook for Singapore*. Washington, DC: The American University.

Williams, Lea E. 1976. *Southeast Asia: a history*. New York: Oxford University Press.

Notes

1. Estimates of the number of regional languages currently used in Indonesia range from 250 to 500, depending on criteria employed to distinguish languages from dialects; in 1972, Indonesia's National Language Institute officially listed 418 distinct languages (Nababan 1985; Stevens 1973). Except in the easternmost province of Irian Jaya (the western half of the island of New Guinea), these languages are generally related through the Malayo-Polynesian language family, but few of them are mutually intelligible (Stevens 1973; Vreeland et al. 1975; Nababan 1985). The majority of these languages are used in the sparsely populated eastern islands by at most a few thousand speakers each. However, several languages on the more populous islands to the west have many more speakers, including Javanese in Central and East Java, 58.8 million; Sundanese in West Java, 22.3 million; Madurese in Madura and East Java, 7.0 million; Minangkabau in West Sumatra, 3.7 million; Batak in North Central Sumatra, 3.1 million; Balinese in Bali, 2.9 million; and Bugis/Makassar in South Sulawesi, 2.8 million (1980 census data in Nababan 1985; see also Peacock 1973; Vreeland et al. 1975; Abas 1978; Nababan 1982). In addition, a significant number of Indonesia's three million Chinese, who reside mainly in the seaports and larger cities, use Hokkien, Hakka, and Cantonese (Nababan 1979; 1982).

2. By 1985, one estimate of Indonesia's population was 167,550,000 (*Britannica Book of the Year, 1986*).

3. At that time, the Chinese comprised over 50% of the population on the west coast of the Malay Peninsula (Le Page 1962).

4. One estimate of Malaysia's population in 1985 was 15,551,000. An estimated distribution of the major ethnic groups in 1983 was 55.8% Malays and 33.3% Chinese; of the 10.9% "others," the majority were South Asians (*Britannica Book of the Year, 1986*).

5. One estimate of Singapore's population in 1985 was 2,558,200. An estimated distribution of the major ethnic groups in 1984 was 76.5% Chinese, 14.8% Malays, 6.4% South Asians, and 2.3% "other" (*Britannica Book of the Year, 1986*).

What National Languages are Good For

Ralph Fasold

Some time ago, Joshua Fishman (1968) introduced several technical terms into the study of the sociology of language. One of these terms, *nationality*, refers to an sociocultural group of a particular type. That is, a nationality has all the properties of an ethnic group, but in addition has developed beyond primarily local self-concepts and concerns, and may also have a larger and more complex level of sociocultural integration than ethnic groups do. It is not necessary, in Fishman's definition, for there to be some polity corresponding to a nationality; many nationalities live within the borders of states governed by other nationalities. If, in fact, a nationality "largely or increasingly" controls an independent political unit, Fishman would call it a *nation*. By this definition, not every country you find on a map of the world is a nation. Some countries, Switzerland is perhaps an example, are not sufficiently under the control of a single nationality to qualify as a nation in this technical sense. *Nationalism*, in Fishman's scheme, is the organization of the beliefs, values and behaviors of a nationality with regard to its own self-awareness. Since nationalities are sociocultural groups, quite independently of whether or not they are in control of a political-territorial entity, nationalism has to do with group pride and awareness, rather than with governing a political unit.

Assuming that we are talking about a nation in Fishman's sense, a country substantially under the political control of a single nationality, then governing is also an issue. Legislative bodies have to formulate and record laws in some language or languages, children need to be educated through the medium of one or more languages, military and police organizations must function in one or another language. These tasks have considerable urgency. They must be carried out on a regular basis or the country will not function, and they are quite different from the concerns of nationalism. Where the political and territorial integrity of a country are the most important issues, Fishman uses the term *nationism*. A language which is used for nationalist purposes, we can call a *national language*. A language used for nationist purposes can be called an *official language*. To overstate the case a bit, a national language can be compared to the national flag. A country's flag functions almost entirely as a symbol. An official language is more like the trackage and rolling stock of a national railroad. It's purpose is more pragmatic than symbolic.

There is a third function a language might serve, although Fishman does not mention it, perhaps because it is so obvious. We might call it the *communicative function*. The communicative function overlaps with the official function, in that it refers to communication among the people in a country, but it also includes the unofficial, unexceptional social interactions of everyday life— chatting over the back fence, trading at the market, yelling at the children and so on. What I hope to isolate by invoking the communicative function, is ordinary talking divorced from any symbolic or identity value a language variety might also have. I realize this is an abstraction, and, like all abstractions, it artificially simplifies the reality that inspires it.

Another notion that I will invoke in this discussion is what I call *naturalism*. Naturalism simply means that we try to determine what is actually happening, regardless of whether what is going on has been officially endorsed by law or constitution. From the naturalist point of view, Guarani has been the actual national language of Paraguay in spite of the fact that it was declared to be a co-national language with Spanish only in 1967. On the other hand, if we consider India as a whole and view the national language issue from the naturalist perspective, we would have to say that Hindi has not yet become the national language, although it was so declared at independence. Whether or how soon a given language will become a national, official or communicative language in the naturalist sense depends heavily on how well suited it is to fulfilling that particular set of functions. The case of former colonies shows the contrast between the requirements of a national language and those of an official language. The language of the former imperial country is usually the best qualified as an official language, at least in the beginning. The governing institutions have most likely been set up in the colonial language and nationist tasks are carried out with the least disruption if the use of that language is continued. On the other hand, the former colonial language is an absolutely atrocious choice as a national language. Nothing could be a worse symbol of a new nation's self-awareness than the language of a country from which it had just achieved independence. Of course, if the national language of the newly-independent *nationality* is the language of the former "mother country," as in the case of English, French, Portuguese and Spanish in various parts of the new world, the colonial language will serve quite well as both national and official language.

In fact, it is popularly and universally considered desirable for the *same* language to serve all three functions. This general inclination to favor a single language for all functions of a nation does have some arguments in its favor. I think it is important conceptually to separate nationalism and national languages from nationism and official languages, and both from communicative languages. However, I do not want to leave the impression that nations typically have one language they use to implement governing tasks with no more emotion or loyalty attached to it than you might have for a hammer; another that inspires loyalty and devotion, but has no communicative use at all, and another or several others that people simply use for chatting with each other. As Fishman (1984) has recently pointed out, where language is concerned, nationism and nationalism are intertwined. The development of national languages is part of the development of a nation as a whole. Pre-developed states are often characterized, among other things by structural compartmentalization (Fishman

1984:42). Compartmentalization tends to be mutually reinforcive by occupation, ethnicity and religion. To cite Fishman's example: "Poles = landholders = Catholics; Ukrainians = peasants = Eastern Orthodox; Jews = petty merchants = Jewish." Language is one more factor involved in compartmentalization, with each group's verbal repertoire contributing to within-group cohesion and to separation from other groups. To the extent that an industrialized society demands the breakdown of this sort of compartmentalization and the establishment of social cohesion at a more inclusive level, the development of a national language (in the naturalist sense) is essential. Even in a nation such as Tanzania, which has declined to attempt to build an industrial society, the development of a national language seems to have been essential to national goals. Tanzania, in fact, is one of the brightest success stories with respect to national language development in a newly independent state (cf. Merritt, Abdulaziz in this volume).

The closest approximation of a pure national language might be Irish Gaelic (or simply Irish) in Ireland, as Rubin (1984:8) has noticed. By the time the Republic of Ireland achieved independence earlier in this century, Irish had receded before English to the point that it was the native language of only a tiny minority. Even as a second language, it was used by a rather small minority of the population. After independence, the new Irish constitution designated Irish as the national language and as the first official language (English was the second). The nation set about a restoration of the Irish language that was designed to increase the use of Irish for official functions, and also to make it the language of ordinary communication for Irish citizens.

Without going into the details, and with the realization that there are those in Ireland and elsewhere who disagree, it seems to me that the Irish government did about all you can expect a government to do to in support of a national language. The primary education system, for example, was brought into the enterprise to such an extent that one Irish observer (O Huallachain 1962:80) sees the system as having 'a double purpose: to give the instruction usually imparted to children up to the age fourteen and to teach Irish'. Yet, the restoration effort, by and large, has either stood still or been slowly pushed backward. The native Irish-speaking

population, only about 3% of the total population at independence, is now less than 1%, only a few tens of thousands of
people. In a survey taken in the late 1960s (O Huallachain 1970),
only 2% said they used the language at home 'all or much of the
time' (this would include second-language users). Only slightly
over half of those who claimed to use the language 'at least
occasionally' said that it was of any practical use to them (most of
the uses they cited were directly related to the restoration effort,
such as helping children with homework). There has been a steady
decline in the use of Irish in education above the primary level, and
the requirement that an Irish competency test be passed to secure a
civil service position—never more than a formality—was abandoned in 1974.

In spite of the bleak results compared to the stated goals of the
restoration effort, I would agree with Rubin that Irish serves as the
national language of Ireland, relating the term 'national language'
to Fishman's concept of nationalism. In a fairly recent large-scale
study of reported attitudes and language use (Brudner and White
1979), it was found that attitudes about Irish were generally
positive, but bore little relationship to reported use of Irish. But
there *was* a close association between attitudes towards Irish as an
ethnic symbol, Irish nationality and Irish speakers. In a small-
sample survey conducted by Lynn Lynch in 1983 among Irish
immigrants to the USA, 22 of 30 respondents objected to the
proposition that Irish is a dead language, and 16 of 29 respondents
agreed that 'Ireland would not really be Ireland without Irish-
speaking people'. Eighteen of 21 said they would like to learn more
Irish. In Ireland, solid support for the maintenance of Irish in the
primary schools seems to be continuing and there has been something of a renaissance in Irish literature, film, theater and music.
There are active organizations, such as the Gaelic League, which
pressure the government to increase its efforts on behalf of Irish
and who encourage the restoration of the language by private
means. In spite of its failure as an official or communicative
language, Irish seems to be serving the nation as a *national* language rather well.

What is a national language good for? It's good as one means
of creating social cohesion at the level of the whole country; an

apparent near-requisite for national development. But at the same time a national language is a symbol of national identity and of a nation's distinction from other countries. Probably no nation, not even Ireland, will ever be fully satisfied with a language that is a national language in a symbolic sense only. But the symbolic sense should never be overlooked. I would dare to suggest that the most frequent single problem in installing a national language has nothing to do with vocabulary expansion, spelling or grammar standardization, the adequacy of the educational system or the presence of an ensconced colonial language. The biggest problem is that there often simply is no language that a sufficiently large majority of the citizens will accept as a symbol of national identity.

References

Brudner, Lilyan and White, Douglas. 1979. Language attitudes: behavior and intervening variables. In: Mackey, William and Ornstein, Jacob eds., *Sociolinguistic Studies in Language Contact: Methods and Cases*, 51–98. The Hague: Mouton.

Fishman, Joshua. 1968. Nationality-nationalism and nation-nationism. In: Fishman, Joshua, Ferguson, Charles and Das Gupta, Jyotirindra eds., *Language Problems of Developing Nations*, 39–52. New York: John Wiley and Sons.

Fishman, Joshua. 1972. *Language and Nationalism: Two Integrative Essays*. Rowley, MA: Newbury House.

Fishman, Joshua. 1984. Language modernisation and planning in comparison with other types of national modernisation and planning. In: Kennedy, Chris (ed.), *Language Planning and Language Education*, 37–54. London: George Allen and Unwin.

Lynch, Lynn. ms. *The Extension of Irish Usage in Ireland*.

O Huallachain, Coleman. 1962. Bilingualism in education in Ireland. *Georgetown University Round Table on Languages and Linguistics 1962*, 75–84. Washington, DC: Georgetown University Press.

O Huallachain, Coleman. 1970. Bilingual education program in Ireland: recent experiences in home and adult support, teacher training, provision of instructional materials. *Georgetown University Round Table on Languages and Linguistics 1962*, 179–93. Washington, DC: Georgetown University Press.

Rubin, Joan. 1984. Bilingual education and language planning. In: Kennedy, Chris ed., *Language Planning and Language Education*, 4–16. London: George Allen and Unwin.